ANOTHER CHANCE MEDIA
presents

BULLYING

BY VINCENT A. SAVAGEAU

BULLYING

Copyright © 2019 by Vincent A. Savageau

All rights reserved. Printed in the United States of America. No part of this work may be reproduced or transmitted in any form or by any means without the written permission from the publishing company.

For information contact:

Another Chance Media

anotherchancemedia.org

Book and cover design by Another Chance Media

ISBN #9780996499958

ABOUT THE AUTHOR

VINCENT A. SAVAGEAU is a man who loves to learn. He has earned many certificates while he has been in prison. Writing courses, communication, leadership, wellness, positive life changes, thinking strategies, and Spanish are just a few of his accomplishments. Vincent participates in kickball and loves to read and of course write. He is well respected among his peers and they appreciate that he is given them an opportunity to share their own experiences. If Vincent had lived in better circumstances and made different choices, he may have accomplished his dream. He would have seen himself as an academic possibly becoming a teacher himself. He loved school and he loved to learn. Things changed for him when he just did not have the proper support at school and at home. Vincent was found to have had a learning disability. If he had the proper instruction, he probably would have gotten the tools he needed to be successful, but for him and so many others that did not happen. Furthermore, he got into situations where he was bullied, and this had a profound effect on his life.

Today, he is a loving, caring person who continuously seeks personal growth, and he has a profound desire to make a difference in this world. Bullying is his first book and hopefully the first of many.

TABLE OF CONTENTS

INTRODUCTION 1

CHAPTER 1 3

CHAPTER 2 35

CHAPTER 3 51

CHAPTER 4 131

CHAPTER 5 153

CHAPTER 6 182

CHAPTER 7 232

CHAPTER 8 271

CHAPTER 9 291

CHAPTER 10 299

INTRODUCTION

THROUGH THIS BOOK, we are going to be talking about bullying insecurities, low self-esteem and the fears behind them. We will also identify why and how one becomes insecure or develops low self-esteem and the fears that trigger these emotions. In this book, I want to show you how and why a victim of bullying can become violent, or even a criminal.

I want to show you how low self-esteem insecurities and the fears of these emotions are directly associated with bullying or put downs. We are also going to learn how to rise above and overcome these negative emotions that leaves one to think that they are weak. We are precious human beings; we were brought into existence as unique intelligent creatures, full of feelings, life and desire to succeed, but we have these stumbling blocks that hinder us from reaching our fullest potential and stop us from being who we really want to be.

So hopefully in this book, through reading my story, you will gain profound insights as well as learn some tools to challenge yourself and conquer these negative feelings that are like rotten apples to the core.

CHAPTER 1

WHEN I WAS A CHILD, I didn't have a care in the world. I was free to believe in whatever I wanted to believe, free to be whoever or whatever I wanted to be. If I wanted to be a bear, I was a bear. If I wanted to be a superhero, I was a superhero. "By the power of Grayskull!" I used to say. I was free, full of fantasies and dreams. But now I'm an adult, with all the responsibilities of what that means, with the weight of the world on my shoulders, life doesn't feel as free any longer. If I began acting like an animal or a character from a TV show, everyone would think I'm crazy.

This is where it all began, what people think of you, what they think of me, of how we can manipulate ourselves through negative self-talk because of what people think of us. Instead of believing in or listening to ourselves, we get caught up in what people say about us. How other people treat us, and what other people do to us. This is where it all begins. This is where you start to lose freedom of who you are, where you start to develop into who the world wants you to be. People are insecure and have low self-esteem for a wide range of reasons, but it is fear that will keep one in a mental cage. Fear of anything will trap your mind. Like a deer blinded by the headlights of a car, you get struck not knowing where to go or what to do. Fear is a distressing emotion, regardless of what we think is real or imagined. Fear is a condition of your mind; a belief that says, "I am helpless, what can I do?" The Random House dictionary says fear is often applied towards something, like two little kids picking on one another.

The child being picked on becomes afraid and frightened, resulting in them shutting down, running, or even resorting to violence themselves. This becomes a scar in that child's life, a mental and emotional wound that can result in life lasting behavioral and social development complications.

Now, imagine this type of abuse, verbal or physical, takes place in a child's school, neighborhood, local community center like the Boys and Girls club or Y.M.C.A. Especially at home, where a child is supposed to be safe, a refuge for children to find peace in. Picture that, I want you to think on that. Keep in mind that it only takes one word, just one word, to hurt an adult's feelings. Think of all the possibilities, the outcomes, the stages of that child's life.

Now tell me, if a child suffers this type of abuse, will this abuse create a negative attitude and faulty thinking that could carry over into adulthood? Sure it will. The victims inflicted by this negative behavior will suffer the most and the longest. This abusive type of behavior inflicted upon another, in my opinion, is the cause and the reason why some develop certain mental health disorders, like bipolar disorder, paranoia and depression. This is where insecurities and low self-esteem come in but we will talk more about these emotions later. Right now, I want to really touch on fear and how this emotion/attitude can and will control you.

<u>EXAMPLE #1</u>: Fear now controls you. Fear, when initiated, enters the mind, then the body. Adrenaline starts to rush through, your heart starts to beat faster and faster, you get nervous, you shutdown, caging yourself into this little box of a life. You become afraid. You ask yourself, "What I can do?" Automatically, we as human beings, avoid what we are afraid of. So we look for shortcuts in life, running from the fear. Not knowing that we are running from ourselves, and last I knew, no one can run from themselves. Some things in life are just impossible.

In the example ahead, you are going to see just how controlling and damaging bullying really is, how it manifests into insecurities, fear and ultimately, low self-esteem. I'm going to tell the story of a child. How he was very anxious to become someone, he wanted to become someone. He wanted to be a great person.

He was a good kid going to school, he loved to learn and at home he did as he was told. He enjoyed to read, write, draw and do artwork. He even liked math. He was fascinated by school and education. He even wrote a book one time about his cat.

Growing up as a little kid, he wanted to be a professor. Knowing full well what a professor means, dressing up in his suit and tie, at just the tender age of 9 years old. He would look in the mirror and think of all the good things he wanted to do with his life, but the teachers felt like he had problem learning.

There was a conference between the mother and the teacher. When the mother heard of this news, she took it very seriously. The teacher suggested that the child attend a single class where the student would receive help on a more personal level. The mother took the advice of the teacher; she took all of the necessary steps to ensure her child would receive the best help that he possibly could. The child didn't learn in this class either, so the mother became very uneasy and displeased with the school. She had her child removed and transferred to another school.

For some reason, the little boy had problems at this school as well. The mother thinking that there might be something wrong with her child scheduled an appointment with a doctor. Before you know it, the little boy was in and out of the appointments with all types of different doctors.

One day, the little boy woke up in the middle of the night asking himself, *"Is there something wrong with me? Am I not smart enough, why do other kids always pick on me?"* Yes, he got picked on; he got picked on a lot. But he never told anyone, not even his mother.

He got picked on for always asking for help. He got picked on for the way he talked. He had a speech and language problem. He could not pronounce certain words correctly and when he was excited or frustrated, he would start to stutter. The other kids would taunt him and tease him. They would call him stupid and call out foul names as he passed by in the hallways. He even got picked on for his looks for he was a very fair looking young man with curly hair and green-gray eyes. Whenever he would stand up for himself, he was punished and sent to stand in the corner at the back of the classroom. Sometimes, he was even sent to detention for not paying attention.

There was this one time, when he was running from these two boys. They would like to catch him alone in the hallway or on the stairs in passing, taking the opportunity to beat him up. Needless to say, the little boy did not know how to fight, he was not a violent child nor did he know how to defend himself. The day he decided to run he lost sight of where he is going and he ran straight into the principal. The principal grabbed him up and asked, "Why are you running through my halls? Who are you running from?" As the two boys passed by, he stayed silent. He didn't say a word. So, he is sent to detention yet again. While he is sitting in detention, he thought to himself, "I am not the bad guy. I didn't do anything wrong. Why do I keep getting punished, when I'm the one being picked on?"

The teacher at school didn't like him either, always treating him lowly. One day, out of frustration, he told the teacher, "I don't like you and I don't like this school." The teacher slammed the desk into the little boy, shouting and screaming at him, telling him to shut up. She made him look face down for the remainder of the class. Not only did the little boy get picked on at school, but he got picked on in his neighborhood too. He was a pretty boy, so all the girls liked him.

The problem was, he started thinking he wasn't good enough; he started thinking he wasn't smart enough. He started really believing he was dumb. But still he tried. He refused to give up, because he liked to learn.

He liked nature. He liked reading and writing, and when the teachers paid attention to him, he soaked it up. One day, he was told that he had Attention Deficit Disorder and a learning disability, so the little boy was transferred to another school. The boy bounced around from school to school until his mother found the correct school with a very good teacher, but the damage had already been done and the bullying didn't stop.

It seemed as if everyone wanted to pick on this little kid, and he was little too. Eventually, he fought back, having his first fight at just 10 years old. He was always afraid though.

So as time went by and he grew, his confidence was replaced by fear, his mind was filled with insecurities, and his heart filled with low self-esteem. Always questioning himself. The boy lived in fear, his mother and step father, who loved the little boy as his very own son, spilt up and got a divorce.

The little boy and his family moved to the projects. He was only 10 years old and already had been through so much. His mother found comfort in another man, a man he didn't like very much. A drunken alcoholic that used drugs and life for the little boy only got worse. No one really knew how this little boy felt, he had no one to talk to, and he held everything inside. But he kept going to school, dealing with all of the day to day pressures that no child should have to go through.

Now, I am going to stop right here. We are going to talk more about this little boy's story throughout the entire book.
Right now we are going to identify 3 things about the boy so far.

1) FEAR: Identify how all of the bullying is affected this child. We know what the norm is, he was afraid of what people thought of him. He even started to question himself. But look past that, reread the story, see how all the name calling and bullying was really affecting him. Look at the negative effects that everything was having on him, between the doctors, school, the kids and the teachers. Can you see what it is doing to him, to his mentality, to his ego? The little boy started to lose sight of who he was, he lost his freedom. He went from wanting to be someone, to just making it through another dayWhy was the boy being bounced around from school to school? Do you think it is because the boy can't learn? Or that he is stupid or is there really another problem going on here. If there is, what is it?Can you see how he was losing himself and a sense of who he wanted to be? How was he being stripped of his own power, how this little boy was humiliated? How in his mind, he was being turned into this frightened, timid little boy.

First, he is bounced around from school to school; he is told he is stupid and dumb when he is just looking for help. Then when he fought for himself, defended himself, he was punished, while the other kids he was standing up to for picking/bullying him got to resume their normal activities. Or look at how he was sent to detention for not paying attention. How about the time the teacher, the adult, the protector slammed the desk into this child and forced him to look face down. Keep in mind that he was in a classroom full of other students. What type of effect do you think this had on him, what type of message was the teacher sending to the other students. Now, can you see the fear, can you see in his mind how he was being broken? This child was only 10 years old and already he is being humiliated and treated as if he is not a human being!

2) THE COURSE THIS BOY HAS TAKEN: Now which direction do you think this little boy's life will go? Reread the story speculate, assume, draw conclusions-the story does have its own. See the mental trauma, and physical abuse. Oh, and for the record, bullying is abuse. Look into his mind, see through his eyes. See if you can feel what he feels. Then ask yourself, if you were this child, what would you do? Now you're sitting there in the classroom. You're being called a punk. You're soft. I don't know why you ask for help. You're just stupid. You'll never be anything.

You tell the kid to shut up and stop talking to you like that. The teacher tells you, "Don't use that language in my classroom, he told me I was stupid." I don't care what he said to you, don't talk like that in a classroom. Now you go stand in the back of the room for that outburst. Now, you're standing there and you're thinking to yourself, you don't care what he said! What form of mind is this child being put in, how is he being controlled, and what should he do?

3) HIS FEELINGS: Remember this section of the book is on fear and how it controls you. Imagine this little boy, this child, he is confused. He feels lost, like he is the only one in the world. He is hurt, his pride is damaged. He has a speech and language problem, so he cannot express himself correctly. The once happy go lucky kid is living in a shell. He is confused because it's the adults that are supposed to protect him. It's the adults that are supposed to stop the children from bullying and being mean to each other. It's the adults that are supposed to provide safety and comfort. So what happens when the adults fail to do so? What happens when the adults turn the other way? What happens when the adults are the ones that are aggressive, abusive and mean? Remember teachers are adults, adults are authority figures.

The little boy started to become violent. He lost respect for his teachers and anyone who tried to tell him what to do, he dislikes. He was so protective of himself that he started to think that everyone wanted to hurt him, so he didn't let anyone near him... the child developed a paranoia, a complex, he is under the impression that only the tough kids get left alone.

Now let's get back to the story!

Living in the projects is no joke, especially for a light skinned, green-grey eyed, young kid. He is made into a target out of the gate. Some might say that the projects turned this little boy out, that street life corrupted him. It is true the projects/street life did play a part in turning this once joyful, happy child into a law breaking criminal. But I am here to tell you, this child's issue started long before he moved to the projects, and any child with these same types of problems started long before a child starts running the streets. That's what the next chapter is all about. But keep in mind the point for this chapter is fear and how we can let what others think about us control our lives, especially a child. They live to please their peers!

The little boy continued to go to school. He was on his way to the ninth grade. Jr high had its ups and downs, but nothing he really wants to remember. The same old routine every day, but there are a few moments he will never forget! Like the time this big kid came up from behind him, put him in a headlock, causing the little boy to pass out from lack of oxygen. While he is unconscious, the big kid poured milk all over the face.

Coming back to consciousness the little boy still remembered his exact words when he walked away. *"You're nothing, you're just a little punk!"*

As the boy got up, taking his shirt off to clean himself up, everybody laughed at him and he couldn't find his glasses. He didn't need his glasses to see how pretty Rose Mary was as she came over to help him and asked him if he is okay.

The boy and Rose Mary became real good friends after this. They called and talked to each other over the phone constantly. After school one day, the boy almost had to fight her boyfriend, he was a junior high school basketball player, who didn't like the boy talking to his girl.

When he approached, the boy asked if there was a problem. The boy didn't like this one bit. Rose Mary was his friend, for some reason he felt strong when she was around. So standing there, he felt every muscle in his body fill with adrenaline that was beginning to rush. His heart beat faster and faster. Face to face, they stared each other down, but no punches were thrown, instead a meet up was set for after school. Now the big kid that poured milk all over the little boy approached the boy, telling him he would have his back.

Now, this confused the boy, because this was the same kid that always bullied him. But sure as the day, he (Jason) was waiting right there for him after school with all of his friends. As they approached the basketball player standing there with all of his friends, the little boy dropped his book bag, taking his stance, ready to fight. The basketball player didn't want to fight. He said, "I'm not going to fight you over some girl. I don't even like her anyway." I believe, if that little boy would have shown up by himself, he would have been jumped and for Rose Mary, that little boy was going to show up by himself.

Jason, who was the bully along with Eli, and the little boy became good friends. They all took the same bus to and from school together. Now instead of sitting in the front, Jason wanted the little boy to sit in the back of the bus with him and the rest of the kids. The boy always wanted to be one of the cool kids, he always wanted to be accepted among his peers, so this felt cool. He really didn't like hanging with these kids because they were a bunch of jerks. Not just toward him, but toward everyone around and for some reason the girls laughed at everything the guys did.

One day, the boy and Jason had words. Jason kept picking on this one little kid, Nathaniel. Jason took Nathaniel's hand held video game, so the boy stepped up and told Jason to give it back and even took the game from him. Jason didn't like this very much.

Long story short, the boy stopped hanging with Jason and Eli and started hanging with Nathaniel instead. He started sleeping over at his house, playing with him and his sister.

Anyway, those moments when the boy felt proud of himself for stepping up to the bully that had always bullied him and even stuck up for his new found friend. There are a few other moments, like the art project, or his first science project, and the birdhouse he made in wood shop but his favorite project of all is the book he wrote about his cat. His mother has that book till this day, but there are so many cold memories of school, like when he attended New North and the way he always sat in the cafeteria alone.

He only made one friend that entire school year. This was the school where the bullying intensified. He was somewhat of a nerd His favorite color was red, so he always had on red sneakers, red hat or a red sweater. Purple is also one of his favorite colors, so you could imagine how much he stuck out. But if you were to ask that little boy, he thought he was cool with his curly hair, green-gray eyes and always coming to school selling pencils. His mother gave him five bucks one day. He took that $5 bucks and bought some football pencils, two of each team, selling them for twenty-five cents each at school. The boy did this until he got beat up along with all of his pencils taken.

This is the same school where the teachers said he had a speech and language problem. Although he got bullied in this school, he really liked this teacher, Miss Gun. Miss Gun was the best teacher he ever had.

Summertime came around and his mother sent him to go stay with his aunt and uncle in New Hampshire. During the summer, he did normal things, like swimming, fishing, camping and he wished and even prayed to God that he could stay there for the rest of his life but he returned home for the beginning of the school year.

School started and he was somewhat excited about attending high school, then he thought about the teachers and wondered if high school was going to be anything like all the other schools he went to. And with that thought, he promised himself he wasn't going to let anyone bully him again, even if he had to fight.

Now, I know what you're thinking here, why didn't he talk to his aunt and uncle? You know kids keep secrets better than any locked door, they are afraid. That's why it is very imperative to have an open relationship and line of communication with your children.

High school was rough, the kids were fast and some of the teachers were a hot mess. Bullying wasn't as distinctive at the high school. Basically, there were two sides to it. You were either tough or you weren't. Of course, if you weren't tough, you became a high school physical and verbal punching bag. Even the girls were nasty there, but the little boy never had problems with the girls, if anything, they were way too fast for him and out of his league. They were always running up to him, touching and playing with him. Of course he liked this.

One day, this big tall giant of a kid decided he wanted to pick on the boy, who is very quickly growing into a young man. His voice had gotten deeper and he had grown a little taller. The tall kid pushed the boy, then called him a punk. This was the first time in the beginning of the year that anyone approached him with a problem. The young boy quickly remembered his promise to himself, then he charged the tall kid.

Instantly, they began punching and throwing each other around that classroom like two wild dogs. The boy even surprised himself when he got the upper hand, hitting the tall kid hard before slamming him into the chairs. After that, the tall kid was done; he didn't want to fight anymore. You are probably wondering where the teacher was, so was the boy.

Word spread fast around school that day, quickly making him enemies he did not want. Not knowing it, he went straight on to the cafeteria. Did I tell you that this boy was somewhat of a nerd wearing glasses? Well, not anymore, they got broke during the fight.

A group of kids were waiting for him at the cafeteria. They didn't hit him, but they made it clear that they would be waiting for him after school, and that they did. They hurt this boy. They hurt him bad and he stayed out of school for a week, allowing him time to heal. He did his best to hide all of his bruises from his mother and the rest of his family, but his little brother caught him in his room with his shirt off while changing his clothes. He lied to his brother and said he got jumped by some neighborhood kids, which really wasn't a lie, he'd been jumped by them before.

When the boy returned to school, he got threatened. There was a knife involved. Needless to say, the boy was afraid for his life. He never returned to school again. Telling or snitching is and was a big NO NO... When you're a kid you don't want to be looked at as a punk and a total tell.

He didn't know what to do. He figured he will deal with his own problems like a man, but how could he deal with his problems like a man when he is not a man. He was just a child-only 13 years old.

We are going to stop again right here. I want you to see what is going on so far.

1. You can see that he is ready to stand up for himself.
2. You can see how what he went through at prior schools is having a major effect on him. You can also see what he went through is controlling him mentally.
3. You can see how this child feels like he is all alone.
4. You can see how he wishes for a better life. Which is most important, you can see how his actions are turning

physical. He is truly a good kid living in a dog eat dog world... Now can you see his feelings of hopelessness?

CHAPTER 2

BULLYING IS A BIG PROBLEM here in America. Young boys and girls in their teens are acting out in frustration and violence all because of bullying. Some boys and girls even resort to suicide. Some are coming to school with weapons committing horrible acts of crime, some of these being murders. This hurts my heart for everyone involved, but these kids are looked at like they are the bad guys, when really, they are the victims... victims of bullying.

Everybody points the finger at the "Crazy psycho came to school and just started shooting everyone". That child's parents are the ones to be blamed, but really that child was the victim. Like I said, my heart hurts for everyone. Mothers are crying all over the news, saying things like, "My son was a great kid" or "He got accepted to college". Other kids are killing themselves, leaving their families behind in confusion for the rest of their lives. Saying things like, "I don't understand, my kid loved chemistry and science", "He wrote me a letter telling me he was gay and nobody liked him so he committed suicide", and our young women are being made a mockery of because they are not the next cheerleader or pretty girl in school. They are nerds wearing glasses that like to read and write.

Another point people don't look at, crime is high in our country. Why? Well, I'm going to tell you why - not only with my words, but with the words of criminals having a hard time in our federal penitentiary system. They are going to tell you with their own words why they became violent, which lead to a life of crime. Why they became menaces to society. I'm pretty sure you heard of all the stories. Poverty, broken homes, addiction to drugs or *I just hung around with the wrong crowds*.

Well, you never heard stories like these before and hopefully you will hear many more. I wish to spark and ignite a flame in many others who will step up and speak out.

We, as people, need your voice to be heard. I call these stories the truth behind the scenes, and we are going behind the scenes. With real criminals that commit real crimes. But before we go there, I want to talk about the freedoms of this country.

People are free to be gay. People are free to color their hair purple or green. People are free to dress however it is they want to dress, and be whomever or whatever they want to be. The freedoms of this country are great. Every day the government and citizens are finding new ways for our country to be free and the constitution protects all of our rights. But what's taking place with our children in our schools and in our streets?

Our communities are taking part long before these matters ever reach a courtroom. How can the rights of our children/young teens be protected if they are dead? Children are being picked on a day to day basis, being harassed and treated like they are not human beings and they are left to their own irrational thinking. But everyone just shrugs it off like it's no big deal.

"You gotta' be tough kid, don't let them see you cry" Or "I will talk to the parents or teachers tomorrow." Well, what happens when you talk to the teacher and nothing happens? What happens when the teachers are the ones bullying? What about that child like the one in the story of this book that is afraid to talk to anyone because he is scared? Oh, it is his fault because he didn't talk to anyone, right? What type of message is being sent out to the young youth of our country today? When we as adults just turn the other way, or we don't take our children serious enough, or how about when we, as adults, are overly aggressive with our young ones?

Or how about when there is no real communication between parents and their children? It is just, "Good morning, have a good day at school, don't be bad, clean your room make your bed and how are your grades?" Children, young kids and teens are naturally secretive. They are taught from the day that they are born that they are children and that they have no place in an adult's face. Separation starts between adult and children from the beginning. They have to earn our respect amongst our position. They are told to stay in their place and this is enforced if need be.

This is true, there are certain areas and things that children are not prohibited doing, but we are only preaching one side of the message. We are not telling our children, "It is okay to come and talk to me. If you are scared, hurt or have a problem or any questions." We think that they are just children and don't have serious problems. WELL YOU'RE WRONG, YOU'RE ALL WRONG, because bullying is a very serious problem.

This is what I have to say, it is not the children that have to earn our respect, but us as adults that need to earn theirs. We need to earn their respect and their trust, before we can ever tell them what to do. If you have children show them that you are true. Show them that you are there for them right or wrong, thick and thin, through and through.

It is instrumental that we go beyond the norm with our young, ones whether our own or others. Talking is a very big deal for children/teens. I don't know about you, but I remember almost everything about my childhood from detail to detail. And let me tell you, whenever I was around adults, I felt like I was around giants with their big hands and faces. It's like always walking around talking about something. I was so afraid to talk to my parents outside of normal conversation. Yeah, I use to ask all kinds of questions, like what is a star and are there people on the moon?

But I felt it inappropriate, even scared to talk about the hairs growing in under my waistline or the first girl I ever kissed. I was afraid because as a child or a young teen, you don't really know what's right or wrong.

You don't think rational you just do it, and learn as you go.

For example, if a little boy walks up and punches another kid in the face, he's not thinking about the impact or the effects that his behavior will have on another person. He is not thinking about the consequences, there is no rational thought, just "Wow, I hit that kid. Now he is going to do whatever I tell him to do. Give me your lunch ticket punk. Wow, I got away with that!" So, he does it again.

Now this is where it gets good, there are laws against adults doing this to each other. If I hit you, you can press charges on me, file a restraining order, see to it that I am convicted and sent to jail. Or even pay fines and hospital bills, etc. Adults are held to a different standard than anyone under age, if anyone under age commits a crime or breaks the law, yes, they are held accountable, but the severity of their crime is held by a different standard. Why? Because they are minors, their thought process is not fully developed. That is why it is prohibited for an adult to sleep with a minor.

The whole point of this is, we have laws in this country, that when enforced, they keep people in line. Laws that protect people, just think if we didn't have laws, the chaos that could ensue. But I can't help but think that with all these laws, there is no direct law against bullies or bullying. There should be a law implemented against bullying and enforced not by a patrol officer or a police department, but by a special unit that is a part of the school department protected by the union that is funded by the Federal Government and the taxpayers of this great nation. I am pretty sure that the American people would agree that having and knowing that their children are safe while attending school and that their children are protected while they are not there would make them feel that much better.

It is time to put an end to the cause and reason why children are committing suicide, murder, dropping out of school, to become nothing but criminals.... all because of bullies. United States of America, we do have a problem, and it is getting worse! I watch the news, world news, and it hurts my heart to know that our children are not safe in our own schools and to know the cause and the reason behind why our children are committing such horrible acts against themselves and others. It shames me, as a human being, seeing this, especially being part of a country that is so free and protected.

We have adults in our school's treating our children like the scum of the earth on top of all the bullying, picking and name calling, it is no wonder why children are turning out to be the worst generation that this country has ever had.

The law, along with the special unit that I am talking about should be there to not only protect and serve these kids from each other but from adults as well. There should be an internal unit not taking sides, but only there to assure the safety between children and staff as well. These young teens should be held accountable for their actions against each other and adults should be held accountable as well.

If one child or a group of children get caught bullying or if a report is filed, the offender should have to perform community service around the school. If the offender refuses, then the parents should be forced to pay a fine of $250 and upward. Depending on the severity of the act/offense committed, if the parents refuse to pay the fine then the child should be suspended until further notice along with a record to be kept of the offender.

If the parents try to place the child/young teen into another school, so that school can and will be put on notice of the offender and the course of action that has taken place. As for adult staff/school teacher, they should not only be fired, but brought up on charges by the state, pending jail time, etc.

As well as recorded as being an official act of child abuse, there should be a record kept on adult staff and school teachers as well. I guarantee, if there was such a unit that existed within the schools, you would see more order and less chaos. You would see more graduates, less drop outs and no more suicides over bullying. There would be no more murders/crimes taking place in our schools, our children should be safe. It is not only the parent's responsibility, but the responsibility of this entire country to ensure/enforce that safety. I hope in this book you will identify how child/young teen can develop a certain persona.

I always hear people say, "Well, I had it bad too" There's no excuses. Well, most kids can't see outside of the 'box'. Most kids can't see a way out. They just see what is before them and people are always so quick to judge. If I can do it, he or she can do it too. If I had to go through that, you have to go through it too... Well, this type of attitude is plain old arrogant, ignorant, stinking, thinking and disgusts me. Anyone who thinks like this should be ashamed of themselves. These are children we are talking about here. Look at our schools, they're falling apart. These are children, young men and young women. There is no one there to help them until it is all too late.

How many more young lives do we need to lose? How many more young lives need to be infected because of this disease? We are supposed to teach the next generation to be better than we were and are. There was no one there to teach me, look at all you went through and look at how hard it was for you. We have to teach the next generation to be better, not just left to suffer the same impending fate.

Bullying used to be looked at as nothing, just a part of everyday life. But it has always been a problem and today you can see it more clearly than ever before.

CHAPTER 3

SO, THIS YOUNG TEENAGER dropped out of high school because he was afraid. Obviously, no one missed him because his mother was never notified and he had been out of school for almost a whole year, but he still practiced his same routine, getting up early in the morning, leaving as he always does. He left into the street with nothing to do. Remember, he is only 13, so he liked to go downtown a lot, walking around, looking at all the different historical sites in the city. His favorite place to hang out was the city's museum, but they always ran him out because it was during school hours.

He was almost through the year and his mother still had no clue that he is out of school. His mother worked two jobs, so when she is home, she was resting up for the next day. After school hours, it is his responsibility to watch his little brothers and his two little sisters, pick them up from their bus stop on the corner every day. Each bus arrived at a different time. One day during the walk back home, these group of neighborhood kids were shouting and screaming all kinds of names at the boy. He kept telling his little brothers and sisters to keep walking faster, don't look back, just keep walking home. They made it home without any other problems, but the boy didn't like that one bit.

One day his little brother, 5 years younger, was outside playing when he came sprinting into the house crying and sporting a black eye. So, the boy, enraged that someone would hit an 8-year-old boy in the face like that, ran outside to look for the punk that hit his little brother, but he didn't find anyone. He told his little brother not to go outside and play with the little kids any more. In his mind, he is not going to let anyone hurt his little brothers and sisters.

In the meantime, this 13-year-old boy ran through his neighborhood looking for this kid that hit his little brother.

He hated anyone that tried to boss him around or tell him what to do. It didn't matter who it was from, policemen to regular people. He had a big problem with authority. On top of that, he taught all four of his brothers and sisters how to fight. He would always sit them together and tell them never let anyone pick on you or treat you any less than what you deserve. He would always tell his sisters how beautiful they were, and to never let anyone mistreat you. He would always tell them, "The whole world is full of scumbags and no one really cares, so you have to be strong." He would tell them, "If anyone ever put their hands on you or is mean to you, you tell me. I don't care who it is, adults or even boys your own age." He would always make them all that promise.

In this chapter, I want to show you how an innocent little boy full of dreams, wonder and the greatest possibilities in the world, can turn into a mean and violent person, or even a criminal. Because violence is criminal, right? I make it clear, taking you through some of the events of the boy's life that led up to him becoming violent. Now there is no excuse, and I will make none for the boy, he chose his path. He could have kept on going to school, dealing with all of the bullying, fighting to make his way, but he chose to drop out of school because he was afraid. He became violent anyway because he is tired of being afraid. With everything built up inside of him, never having anyone to talk to and as he got older, he felt like he had to be strong, not only for his mother, but for his siblings as well.

Being that he was not yet a man, he didn't know how to deal with his own problems; he didn't know how to talk about them. He didn't know how to express himself. Remember the boy was picked on for his speech and language problem. Also, keep in mind, the point of this book is bullying and how it affects young children, young adults and young teens, how most kids who become criminals and outlaws of society were once victims of bullying. I want to show how dangerous and mentally disturbing bullying really is.

Most criminals, as well as young teens, have a problem with authority. Most people think it is because of music or television. Well, these may be an influence on our young minds, but music and television are not the soul and root cause of kids and young teens becoming criminals. Bullying is and I can prove it, not only with the true stories of this little boy but als/o the true stories of real criminals. We will hear from these real criminals in Chapter 6.

And then you can tell me whether I am right or wrong. I am here to show you by talking to you as a people, that bullying is not only the cause of suicides, murder, crime but that bullying is a direct cause for most of our violent criminals in this country today. You may not agree with me, but by the time you are done reading this book, you will feel the full weight and impact of the true stories that take place every day right here in our very own backyard. Welcome to America! Now, I want you to identify 3 more things about the boy so far. Keep in mind we haven't even touched on his low self-esteem, or his insecurities... although you can see them throughout the story. But for right now, the 3 things I want you to focus on is what's happening with this boy.

1. He is going from being a loving, kind-hearted kid to becoming a violent individual.
2. He is losing his values of humanity, as well as his trust in people.
3. How a young teen really doesn't have any rational thought process.

Throughout the book, I will always refer you to go back and reread the story because I want you to have a clear understanding of not just one point, but of the whole message in its entirety. It is very important that you see the negative transitions of a once nonviolent, joyful, happy little kid. How he grows to be such a monster and is now an outcast of society. While everyone else is living their lives, he is the only one still suffering. He was suffering then and he is suffering now.

Some might say that it is his fault by how he turned out. He accepts the weight and responsibility of his own actions. The sole purpose of him writing this book is to reach out to America... to plead that you be more hands on with your young ones of this great nation... that you apply yourselves effectively; pay more attention to our young people so they don't make the same mistakes and bad choices that I did... to find themselves sitting in a prison cell only to be crushed and broken by the memories of their past and tormented by all the possibilities of a "could-be" future. We need to protect our children and youth because they are our future. The future of this country lies in their hands. Our ancestors did not fight and die for our liberties just so we can bury them.

And I'm talking about everyone's ancestors who played their part in building and creating a marvelous, wonderful homeland...whether they are black, white or brown. Our ancestors have fallen and died for our freedom to make this country a great nation. The blood sweat and tears that are soaked deep in the soil along with all the prayers that rose up, to the highest mountains, are on our hands... for all who want to share in the American dream of justice, rights and equality...This country has to be the greatest country in the world because it doesn't matter your beliefs, ethnicity, religion or your cultural background or where you come from because you are free to be whomever or whatever you want to be.

So, to be such a great nation, why is it that our young ones are turning out to be so troubled? You really believe it is because of music or television, I don't. I think it is bigger than that. But no one is listening; kids are left alone to believe, as I once believed many years ago, that no one cares and that we are left in a world all alone.

1. While law enforcement of America is busy fighting crime, criminals are pouring in by the hundreds and they're getting younger and younger with each passing year. So, what is the problem? is crime the problem? We must look to

the pure root of the infection that is the only way to cure any disease. The cure is adults, schools, community centers and neighborhoods. We are so caught up in minding our own business that we don't realize there is a big difference in being nosy or snooping in someone's private life than there is in calling your neighbor to say,

"Hey, your son or your daughter is doing this or doing that and I was thinking about getting together with other parents in the neighborhood so we can come up with a parent child watch system that will safeguard our children." I believe one simple phone call like this can save our children, one child at a time.

The communication level between adults at this day and age is very poor and I don't respect it. But this is what you get when you have children having children and with that, please encourage your young adults to use safety when it comes to sex. This is 202, ladies and gentlemen, so you must communicate with your children on all levels not just one. Don't be shy, scared or bashful. Just jump right in. Once your children see that you're not scared, then they won't be scared either. Remember children are very intelligent; they are a little me and you. They respond off of our actions.

What are you left to do? I understand that everyone loves their own privacy, but damn we are all brothers and sisters at the end of the day. And these are children/young teens and young adults that we are talking about here. It's a sad tragedy for some who only have their memories of what their child used to be, all because of bullies. But the sword is double edged for all families involved of such heinous acts of brutality that we see and hear about every day... whether it is the family of the victim or the families of the bullies. This is an issue that takes deep thought, but does it really require that much thought? I don't think so.

Now, I'm not saying we can change the whole world in one day, but things will change if you put forth the effort, one day at a time. It's all on the adults to take time, make time for your children, but take steps 1,2,3 even further. Make it your priority to talk/build some type of relationship with your neighbors. Get to know the parents of the community. Get involved socially with other parents of your child's school. Hey, you never know when you might meet a good friend. Sometimes, it isn't enough to just talk to your children, but it is enough to talk to the other parents. To know them, who they are, even if you don't like the other parent or parents. It's nice to be able to pick up the phone and say "Hello Mr. or Mrs. Jones, I need to talk to you about your son or daughter".

This is just the first step. The second and third steps are to know the coach, the teachers, the principal and even the counselors at the local community centers. This is how you protect yourself as well as your children. Just to know who someone is, what they are all about, and who they are as a person is so powerful that people underestimate the power of just knowing!

We do have weapons people, natural weapons as human beings that we can use to safe guard ourselves our families, our children, but we take for granted these weapons every single day of our lives. You know what these weapons—communicating, knowing, learning, teaching—are all very powerful tools.

Now, I know it is hard on single parents, both women and men alike. Especially being that most of our single parents are women, so please safeguard yourself and your family. Use the tools with your children, those around you directly or indirectly and I guarantee you, even if you don't see effective change in those around you, you will definitely see effective communication within your very own family.

Now, I'm going to give you some scenarios. You can play with these scenarios in your mind. Think of all the possibilities, the what if's, the ups and downs, the do's and don'ts, and put yourself in any one of the character's shoes and ask yourself, "What would you do?" Now, I know you're not going to do the same exact things. You may not even agree, but one thing you will notice is that if the tools are being used effectively and the road blocks of poor communication are being broke down. Remember, there are always two sides to every story.

In these scenarios, you are going to see both sides, but more importantly the side that leads a young teen to commit murder or suicide and become a violent outcast, a criminal of society. You can actually envision this through the entire book. The proof is in my story as well as many others. Just like me or should I say, this turned out just like me.

SCENARIO #1: Mr. and Mrs. Smiles are effective parents demonstrating as well as utilizing the four poster tools of communicating with their children, knowing their children, learning of their children and teaching their children of personal space and comfort zones. Now Mr. and Mrs. Smiles know most of their neighbors pretty well. They attend all of the children's school events and are deeply involved in neighborhood functions... which means that they not only know the principal, the teachers and the coaches of their children's schools but they know a lot of the parents along with their children. Mr. and Mrs. Smiles also use the four power tools with these individuals, knowing of them, who they are as people, learning from them what they like, what they don't like about them.

They focus on teaching these people about their family so that these people/individuals know what to expect from them and their family. Last, but not least, their aim is effectively communicating with all of these people on an individual basis or in a group setting, always showing a high level of respect and integrity. These safeguard Mr. and Mrs. Smiles and their family by being very well known, knowing who they need to know and what they need to know with all of the barriers broken, they have the right to approach any one of these people on a very confident and comfortable level.

Now, let's say Mr. and Mrs. Smiles' son, Timothy, is being bullied by Mr. and Mrs.

Bishop's son, Jake. Timothy informs his teacher as well the principal of the school, because this is what his parents teach him to do. He also told his parents about the situation. Now the Smiles have a power network set up, so everyone is notified and the situation is brought to a resolution. Now, let's say Mr. and Mrs. Smiles don't have this power network setup, they don't utilize any of the power tools and they don't take the time to get to know any of their neighbors or anyone at the school. In this scenario, communication of any type of relief or resolution is very poor. There is no structure except for outside of the American Dream. Unfortunately, Timothy goes to school, he gets bullied, he's frustrated because he doesn't know what to do.

Now, let's say Timothy not only got bullied by other students or even kids in the neighborhood, but also by one of his teachers or other teachers at the school. The parents don't even know this teacher or anything about this teacher and are stressed because there is no power network setup. What do you think would be the outcome in this setting? Timothy grows up keeping all of his frustration balled up inside of him and the process repeats itself with his own children. Timothy commits suicide because he doesn't know and was never been taught how to deal with these types of frustrations.

Another scenario might be that Timothy comes to school enraged and murders these bullies along with many other innocent people. This is the cold-hearted truth ladies and gentlemen. Every single one of these outcomes we hear about every day through the media. To some of you reading this book, this is a sad truth. But this is not the norm. The norm is what we don't see, but we see and hear about it every single day, hmm. I don't think there has ever been a link between the two behaviors up until this day. And that is kids, young teens turning into violent criminals, joining gangs as a direct result of bullying. Let me explain and then I will give you another scenario where the results are exactly just that, a criminal lifestyle, of gangs, drugs and violence.

Like I said before, you may not agree, but by the time you finish reading this book you will have a different view and opinion of what bullying really means. Okay, here's how a victim of bullying becomes violent or a criminal but first, before we get too far off topic, let me just say, you must remember that we, as human beings, are animals of this planet, regardless of how intelligent we are, or how much we have evolved and advanced over the years. There is no way in the world that we can or should denounce or forget our true nature. Take any animal in the world, box them in, they will become violent. Their instincts of survival kick in. We all have these instincts of survival to procreate, to mate, to protect, to eat, to feed. Some of us are more in tune with our instinctive ways, while some of us have more control over ourselves. But nevertheless, we are all animals, but being an animal is something that we all have in common. It is something that every species on this planet recognizes through any encounter and from the beginning of our time on this planet, it has always been, only the strong and the dominate and the smart will prevail. Before anyone had thought about building a house, wrapping their body up with clothes, we all, every single last human being on this planet, started out living in the fields, hunting, eating, sleeping, naked under a tree or in a cave, just like every other animal on this planet. The difference between us and other animals is we understand reason.

We are mankind, mankind being our title. It's just like saying a lion is a feline. The lion is the name of the animal, feline is its title. Feline is the word that is used to express or cover all of its kind. We are all animals with the title of our species being mankind/human being. Our name for each individual species is Greek, French, African, Chinese, and American and so on. I reiterate that we are a species/animal of this planet and you should never denounce your true nature, instead understand yourself. Trust your instincts that will one day save your life. Now let's get back to the story.

A victim of bullying becomes violent or a criminal. Why?

1. Because there is no structure in the home.
2. There is no communication or lessons being taught on how to deal with or handle bullies and believe me, telling your kid to go and sock somebody in the face is not the right lesson, unless it is a means to physically defend and protect them. But at the same time do you really want your kid socking someone in the face for the rest of their lives? No, you don't. So, this is

where politics come in, remember the 4 power tools I spoke of earlier.
3. Feelings of frustration, being all alone, this falls back on communication. Remember ladies and gentlemen that it is hard for an adult to talk about their problems for fear of the unknown or not knowing. Imagine how it is for young adults, teens or even children. It's ten times scarier, ten times harder and don't forget we were all once children, teens and young adults. We should understand and know how hard it is, empathize with your children and have empathy for others. We know what it's like or have you lost your way, forgetting who you are, where you come from?
4. Peer pressure, indirect or direct peer pressure will get the best of anyone

especially a young child or young teen; this goes back to the four power tools. Now, I can sit here and go on and on of reasons why a victim of bullying can become violent or a criminal. You will see clear as day in the stories of the interviews of the hard convicts who were more than obliged to be a part of the spark of change in the young minds of our nation. Before I close out this chapter, here is the scenario, where a good kid turns towards violence to protect himself, and then ultimately starts using drugs and before he knows it, is knee deep in a life of organized crime.

We all know Timothy from the last scenarios. We envisioned him with the four logical outcomes. But this is one outcome, we did not see coming. Little Timmy gets bullied on a day to day basis, he is small, he is tiny, he does not know how to fight or defend himself. He wants to talk to his father but he is afraid of what his father might say or do. So, one day there is this kid, we'll call him Billy, Billy sees little Timmy getting beat up. Billy runs these bullies off and takes little Timmy under his wing. Billy tells little Timmy, if you stand up to them, they won't bother you anymore. "But I don't know how to fight." little Timmy says.

"Come on, I will show you what to do." says Billy. "Put your fist up like this." Billy throws his fists up, clenching both of his hands. Standing in a boxer form, he swings a few punches. Then he tells Timmy, "Now swing at my palms." Billy holding his palms face up, he tells little Timmy, "Hit me as hard as you can." Timmy swings with all of his might. "Good, that was good", says Billy. "Now imagine my palm is someone's face." "But I can't hit someone in the face!" little Timmy says.

"Sure, you can, it's either that or you continue to get your ass kicked by those other kids every time they see you. I'm not going to be there every time to save you, and by the looks of you, you probably get picked on a lot in school too! What school do you go to?"

"I go to City High."

"Oh yeah, you're getting beat up a lot! Look bro you got to change your look, you look like a nerd, which makes you an easy target. You see how I'm dressed? This hoody, these jeans, my boots, they make you look tough, if you look tough, these punk kids won't mess with you. But it's not enough to look tough though. You have to be tough too. If they find out that you are a fraud, then you make yourself look stupid! Then, there go the rest of your high school years, down the wussy drain. And don't wear your backpack over both shoulders like that, leave your pack over one shoulder, it makes you look cool. It fits the whole profile."

"Billy?"

"What's up little Tim?" said Billy.

"Why are you helping me?"

"Because I hate bullies, and you're a cool little dude, you just don't know it yet. I noticed you a few times hanging around the basketball court. Listen little Tim, I gotta' run, I got a date with this smoking hot girl. So, I will see you tomorrow, and remember, fist up and work on that jab."

"Hey Billy, Thanks man." Little Timmy goes home happy he made a new friend. When he made it home, he asked his father to take him to the mall and buy him a new pair of boots and a hooded sweatshirt.

"Sure, why not, anything for my boy." the father says.

At home, before bed, he works on his jabs a little bit; throwing punches this way and that. He does a little over a hundred push-ups, looks in the mirror and feels like a brand-new man. Tim goes to sleep with all of the confidence in the world. The next day he is up early and ready for school.

His mother and father see how he is dressed, they look at each other and his mother says, "Timothy, why are you dressed like that? You go upstairs and change them clothes right now!"

Tim says, "Mom, I'm not a little boy anymore, I'm in high school and don't call me Timothy anymore my name is Tim."

"Hey don't use that tone with your mother! But he's got a point honey; he is in the ninth grade now."

"Look mom and dad, I gotta' go or I'm going to be late for my bus."

"Yeah alright, but we are going to talk more about this when you get home." says his mother.

When Tim is out the house, Mr. Smiles looks at his wife and says, "Baby, it's okay. It's just a phase. It will pass, he is young, he doesn't know which way to go.

Give him some time, he will grow out of it. Eventually, he will find his own way. Look, I love you baby. I will see you later, I gotta' go or I'm going to be late too."

At school, Tim is definitely getting treated different, he is acting different too. His posture is erect, his swag is cool, and he walks with confidence. At the end of class, Tim bumps into his bullies. Tim looks them up and down, then keeps walking. The pack of punks is hesitant to approach him, but the leader of the bunch is not buying it. He approaches little Tim and calls him a punk-sissy boy.

The bully pushes Tim so hard that he goes flying into the lockers with a crash. That got everyone's attention. All eyes are locked on Little Tim now; just a few minutes ago he was walking with all of the confidence in the world. Now, everyone wants to see what he is going to do.

Little Tim gets up to his feet and says, "Only a punk, pushes someone, when they are not looking."

Now, Tim is scared a little, because this is the same kid that punched him so hard in the stomach on the first day of school, that he puked up his breakfast from that morning. But he remembered what Billy told him, so he put his fist up and told the bully, "You're nothing but a punk." The bully got mad that this tiny little kid called him a punk.

He told Tim, "You're the punk, now I'm going to kick your ass." The bully charged Tim with all of his might; Tim is so scared that he threw a jab hitting the boy square in the face. The force from the bully charging and little Tim throwing a punch sent both kids stumbling backwards, but little Tim was still standing on his feet.

The bully fell to his knees with a busted nose. Now, this made little Tim feel confident, so he threw his fist back up seeing that he did some damage from just one punch. The bully was mad as hell and knew that if he doesn't beat this little kid, he is going to lose his respect and the authority that he has had over the other kids. He thought about telling his boys to help him, but he knew he has to beat this kid on his own. Calling for help would just make him look soft.

He got up to his feet looking little Tim square dead in the eyes and said, "That was a lucky punch, you wanna' try that again." Both kids squared off, the bully hesitantly stepped forward just a little bit, little Tim matched his step but took one step to the side and threw a hard right. The bully threw his hands up to block the punch and little Tim kicked him smack dead in the stomach. The bully doubled over grabbing his stomach in pain, leaving his face wide open. Little Tim hit him flushed on the side of his chin, and knocked the bully out cold. Everybody is amazed at what this little kid just did, that's what he looked like, a little kid. Tim grabbed his pack and threw it over one shoulder and just walked away.

This girl came up to him and said, "Wow, where did you learn how to fight like that?"

"I learned the kick from watching TV; I learned the punch from my friend Billy."

"Wow, that was awesome! Well, my name is Amy. Call me."

"Okay, Amy I'll do that."

"Hey, what's your name?"

"Little Tim."

"How about I just call you LT?"

"LT? Yeah, LT, I like that. That's cool." Tim went home with a big head; he saw his father and remembered that his father wants to talk.

"Hey, son, we need to talk." says his father.

"Sure, what's up dad?"

"What's going on with you, what's up with this new attitude and new look you have."

"Nothing dad, I am in high school now. I'm not 10 years old anymore, I am growing up and mom is still trying to dress me."

"Alright, well I understand another five or six years you are going to want to move out and find you own place away from us old folks. You're turning into a young man, and you're ready to start making decisions for yourself. Just as long as you don't get yourself into any trouble, and as long as you're living under this roof with me and your mother you are going to respect the house rules. You understand!"

"Yes, sir."

"Good now go in there and talk to your mother and make sure you apologize for this morning."

"Yes, sir."

The next day, LT wet to school and found that the bully was there outside with all of his friends, waiting on him. "Me and you are going to fight again." the bully said. "This time I'm going to beat you up. If I don't everybody in this school is going to think I'm soft. And I can't have that."

"Alright, you want to fight again, we can fight again."

But what LT doesn't realize is it is a setup, all the boys are going to jump him. As soon as he takes his first punch, they are going to beat him down and that is exactly what they did. Tim goes home with a black eye and a few bruises on his back and sides. He doesn't want his mother or father to see him like this, so he tries to sneak in through the back door. He knows his father is home because he works a regular 8-hour shift at a gas station.

Although he is the manager, he works this shift because there is no one else to cover it. And he likes having the evenings to spend with his wife. His mother works at a restaurant. She is a first supervisor. Sometimes she doesn't make it home until 5 or 6 o'clock. So, there is a possibility she is not there. As he is making his way through the back door, down the hall pass the kitchen, his father is sitting right there in the living room. He needs to pass the living room to make it to the stairs. So, he just walks right on through. "Hey, dad." he said as he passes the entranceway to the living room.

"Hey, Tim, how was school today?"

"It was okay, just another regular day."

"You wanna' come in here and watch the game with me?"

"Na, I am gonna go outside and play some basketball with my friends."

"Alright, just make sure you're back in time for dinner, okay?"

"Yes, sir." Dinner, LT forgot about dinner. For a second, LT thinks about telling his father what happened, then feelings of guilt and shame ride all over him. So now he is stuck, he doesn't know what to do. Tim can't miss dinner because his mother will just come and check on him anyway. So, he put on his sunglasses and he goes outside. As soon as he bent the corner for the park, he sees Billy. Then he thinks, Billy will know what to do.

"Tim, what's up little bro! I heard about what you did yesterday. Those were some killer moves you put down on the wannabe punk, Jake. Everybody is talking about it, even over in my school they're talking about you, bro! You're like the high school champ right now and you didn't even make it out of the ninth grade yet. The girls are gonna' be all over you now, Tim! So, what's up, why are you wearing those glasses?"

"They jumped me, Billy."

"What!"

"Yeah, Jake and his boys jumped me this morning. He said he wanted to fight again, so I said, okay sure we can do it. As soon as I threw the first punch, they all jumped me, bro. My eye is all busted up, and my back and my sides are all bruised. I don't even know what I am going to do, and if my mother or father see me like this, it's over, I don't know what they will do. The last thing I need is my parents mad at me, bro!"

"Alright listen! This is what you are going to tell your parents. You are going to walk in that house like everything is cool, you're going to tell them that you got that black eye playing basketball. You and another kid jumped up at the same time and you got hit by his elbow on the way down."

"Yeah, that's sounds good. I can pull that off! But what about Jake and his boys, what am I going to do about them."

"Hmm, my older brother goes to City High. I would have gone there myself, but my girl goes to Central. So, I told my grandmother to transfer schools. But come on, I am going to take you to my house and introduce you to my brother. But I gotta' warn you, my brother smokes that funky stuff, so he can be a little weird sometimes."

"That's cool man, my cousin does the same thing."

"What's up with your cousin bro, he doesn't have your back?"

"Man, my cousin lives way across town; that fool doesn't even go to school. He got kicked out of so many different schools that nobody wants him!"

"Yeah, well it would be wise to call your cousin and tell him what's going on, he sounds like a hard case. Anyway, come on, this is my house right here. But be quiet, my grandmother spends most of her time in the living room. She's probably sleeping."

"Your grandmother lives with you, bro?"

"Naw, man, we live with our grandmother. Our parents died a long time ago in a car accident. Hey, Nana, you're awake, do you want some water? No, I'm fine. Who is this you have with you?"

"Hello, ma'am. My name is Tim."

"What kind of name is Tim?"

"I'm sorry; my full name is Timothy Smiles!"

"Timothy Smiles, now what's wrong with that?"

"Nothing, I just like being called Tim!"

"You, young ones nowadays, you're always wanting to change something about yourselves. You should learn to accept and love yourself for who you are. Well, you boys go do what you came here to do, but Billy, no company past seven."

"I know grandma; we are just going to talk to Bobby."

"You better not be going to smoke none of that funky stuff. I know what your brother does. You better not be smoking that stuff too. And tell that pretty girlfriend of yours she needs to come by here more often and keep an old lady some company."

"Alright grandma, I love you, holler if you need me, okay? Come on Tim, let's go upstairs. Oh, and that is where I got that word from "Funky stuff", my grandmother, she always calls it that." (knock, knock) "Yo, Bobby open up man!"

"Yo what's up Billy, who's this?"

"This is the kid everybody is talking about. Tim meet my brother Bobby, Bobby meet Tim."

"What's up, little bro? Yeah, I heard of you only in the ninth grade and already making a name for yourself. That's a good way to start off the high school year. You smoke?"

"Na man, I'm cool."

"Alright, well what's going on, I know my brother didn't bring you all the way over here just to meet me. And you don't smoke so, what's up?"

"Well, it's kind of complicated Bobby, Tim got himself into more trouble than he can handle and it is some of my fault."

"Your fault how is that?"

"Well, I'm the one that told Tim here to stand up for himself. I gave him some good advice, but I didn't think Jake and his crew was going to jump him. He is more of a coward than I thought he was. On top of that, I caught Jimmy and his boys messing with Tim a few days ago, that's how I met Tim, and ran them pansies off. But Tim is all by himself out here, I mean he has his mother and his father but that's it."

"So, you come to me for help is that it?"

"Yeah man, we come to you for help bro, because Tim is my boy and you are my brother and you know how it is." "If you beat up one bully the rest of them punks are going to gang up on you and if you don't do nothing about it, then everyone is going to think you're soft and my boy Tim here isn't soft. He kicked that dudes butt fair and square."

"Alright, I'm going to take care of it. But you're gonna' owe me one, the both of you. Let Tim meet me on the right side of the school at 7:30 AM in the morning and don't be late."

"Alright man, I will be there."

"Hey, Bobby."

"What's up, Tim?"

"Thanks, Man."

"You know you little dudes shouldn't be out here, fighting, you should be taking some girl out to the movies."

"Yeah, your right bro, but some people just out looking for trouble and they always make trouble with the people looking for none."

"Ah, man speaking of girls! Amy gave me her number yesterday after I beat up Jake."

Amy? What does she look like?"

"Well, she's tall, long brown hair and she is always wearing these little skirts."

"That's my girl's little sister, Tim. You better be careful little buddy. She might be a little out of your league. She is one grade ahead of you."

"Hey, Bobby."

"What's up, Tim?"

"Since that is your girl's little sister, maybe me and you can double up, huh?"

"I don't think you're ready to ride with me, Tim, I do big boy stuff."

"Man, I'm only four years behind you, what's big boy stuff?"

"The fact that you have to ask that question tells me that you're not ready. Go pop your first cherry, then maybe, maybe me and you can go kick it. Anyway, I gotta' get ready; me and my girl are going to the cinemas."

Outside during the walk back home, Billy makes sure he reminds Tim of what he is going to say to his parents. "Yo', Tim, you remember what you're gonna' tell your parents, right?"

"Yeah, I remember."

"Ay, Tim look over there, it's Jimmy and his boys."

"Hey, little Timmy, we heard you got your butt kicked today by Jake and his boys, Billy can't protect you all the time can he, you little fuckin freak. Don't worry, we will be seeing you soon. We know where you live now."

"Hey, back off."

"Aw, fuck you, Billy!"

"How about you come say it to my face, Jimmy?"

"Don't worry, your day is coming soon too. Your brother won't be around to protect you forever. Isn't he going to college next year?"

"What was all that about, Billy?"

"Ah, I kicked his ass last summer."

"You kicked Jimmy's ass last summer?"

"Yeah!"

"His boys didn't jump you?"

"Well, my brother and his brother play on the same football team. They've been good friends although high school and they were both right there when we fought. But by the time they broke it up, I had already slammed Jimmy in the mud and was on top of him like a bulldog. Apparently, he didn't let it go and to hear he has waited for my brother to go off to college so him and his boy can make a move on me is something, I didn't expect. I thought our beef was over a long time ago."

"Well, what are you gonna' do now, are you gonna' tell your brother?"

"Na, this is something I gotta' handle on my own."

"Well, if you do something, I am going with you."

"Tim you got yourself in enough trouble as it is, you got good parents that love you and my brother is going to take care of that situation with Jake and his boys, tomorrow."

"Yeah, well, just like you, I don't have anybody else when your brother leaves. So, the way I see it is, it's just me and you. If it wasn't for you, I would never had stepped up to Jake and I would have never got Amy's number. So, from this day on, I am your brother. Whatever you go through, I go through it with you, and that's it."

"Alright, I appreciate that Tim, well here's your house. Come on in, I'm going to introduce you to my parents. It's still early it's only 6:30, so we got time to hang out."

"Aw man, are your parents are gonna' trip?"
"Nah, man, they're cool. They don't really do much except go to work and come home. Sometimes they go out on the weekends. Hey mom! dad!"

"We're in here in the kitchen."

"Mom, I got one of my friends with me."

"Timothy, what happened to your eye?" says his mother.

His father said, "Boy, you better not be out there fighting."

"No, sir"

"And who is this you have with you?"

"This is Billy, Billy meet my parents, Mr. and Mrs. Smiles."

"Hello."

"Tim, you didn't say you were bringing company with you," says his father.

"Oh, it's okay, I will fix him a plate. He can have dinner with us," said Mrs. Smiles. "Come on; take off your jacket and hang it up over there, if you're going to hang out with my son then you are going to eat at the table like family."

"Yes, ma'am."

"Oh, I like your friend, Timothy. He has manners."

"Come on, Ma!"

"Oh, that's right, you are a big boy now and you want to be called Tim. I understand you are growing up, so how did that happen to your eye?"

"Just playing basketball. Me and this kid went up for the basketball at the same time. I got hit in the eye, it's no big deal."

"Alright, well you better not be getting into any trouble out there."

"No, ma'am."

"And you, you live around here?" his father asked Billy.

"Yes, sir. I live right up the street with my grandmother."

"And your parents?"

"My parents died in a car accident when I was five."

"Oh, I am sorry to hear that. So, it's just you and your grandmother?"

"No, I have an older brother, his name is Bobby."

"And does he live with you and your grandmother?"

"Yes, sir."

"Oh, okay, well Tim you got the dishes tonight, your mother is pooped and I took out the garbage."

"Aw, come on dad! You know I'm supposed to take the garbage out."

"Well, yeah, me and your mom are the only ones with jobs around here, so don't go trying to get yourself out of this one. Besides, when was the last time I asked you to do the dishes?"

"Alright, alright! I'll do them."

"Billy, what time does your grandmother expect you home?"

"By 8:00, sir."

"Okay, just let me know when you're ready to go and I will give you a ride."

"Oh, that is okay, Mr. Smiles, I only live a couple of houses up the street."

"You sure?"

"Yes, Sir."

"Alright, it's your feet."
"Hey, Tim, I'm going to take off and go see what Jimmy and his boys are up to before I go home."

"Hold on, man, I will come with you."

"Na, it's cool man! I'm not gonna' do nothing, I'm just gonna' check them out."

"Alright, but I'm gonna' come check on you in the morning before I go to school."

"Okay, I will see you then."

The next morning, "Hey, Tim, come on in."

"Billy, listen, I called my cousin last night like you said. I explained everything to him.

"Yeah, what did he say?"

"He said we need to start our own crew."

"Start our own crew?"

"Yeah man, start our own crew!"

"Dude! This isn't the movies, Tim!"

"I know Billy, this is real life man and like it or not, You and I can't beat up Jimmy and his boys by ourselves, so we need to do something. Besides, those punks are always running around here picking and bullying on somebody. I hate those dudes, bro!"

"Alright Tim, I am going to think about it. But right now, you need to go meet my brother at school."

"What! Your brother already left for school?!"

"My brother leaves every morning at six so he can meet up with his boys and girls, so they can all go to school together."

"His boys? See man, even your brother got a crew."

"That's different Tim; they all go to school together."

"Yeah, but I bet they got each other backs if something goes wrong."

"Go to school Tim, we will talk later."

"Alright, I will see you later then. But think about it, bro, that is what we need."

"Yo', when I said be on time, I didn't mean exactly on the minute. You were supposed to be here like 10 minutes ago, Tim."

"It's not my fault man my bus was running late."

"Everybody, meet the freshman that beat Jake's ass the other day."

"Hey, what is up little bro, what's your name?" "Tim, but you can call me LT."

"He's kind of cute. If you were just one year older, I would take you for a ride."
"Lindsay, chill he is talking to Amy, my girl's little sister."

"What! You're talking to my little sister?" Bobby's girl says.

"Hey, all the more reason I would take him for a ride and teach him a thing or two," says Lindsay.

"Alright Tim, I told you I would fix this for you. I got all my boys here; this is half the high school's football team. So, what's it gonna' be, it's your play kid."

"Well, I wanna' beat Jake's ass again, fair and square."

"Okay and we will rough his boys up a little bit. Put a good scare in them. After today Jake and his boys, won't even look at you."

"You know what you need LT? You need to make some friends around here." says one of the football players.
"You know some boys of your own."

"I just did. You guy are my boys, and Lindsay I'll take you up on that ride."

"Oh, he's fresh! Jill you better watch out and your little sister might get hurt with this one."

"Yo'! There's Jake, right there." What's up LT? What you wanna' do?"

"Come on, I'll show you what I'm gonna do."

"Say LT, look boys if it isn't the little turd, we kicked the shit out of yesterday."

"You wanna' kick the shit out of me again?" says LT. "Sure, why not? Come on boys, let's get him!"

"Hold on, Jake. There's not gonna' be any of that today."

"Hey, this doesn't have anything to do with you, man! Our beef is with him."

"Well, if you got a problem with LT, then you got a problem with me."

"Yeah, if you got a problem with Bobby, then you got a problem with the rest of us."

"Hey, you guys are seniors!"

"Yeah and I'm the captain of the football team and this is my line."

"Man, we're not afraid of you guys."

"You're not afraid?"

"Hell no, man."

"Alright, since you're not afraid, and then fight LT, here, by yourself."

"Alright, I'll do that."

"Hey, Jake, these dudes are gonna jump us the same way we jumped him."

"No, they're not they are just trying to scare us."

"What's up, Bobby?!"

"As soon as Jake and LT start fighting, you and the boys grab his crew and teach them punks a thing or two about bullying."

"Got you, bro. LT yeah, you better kick this guy's ass!"

"I will."

"Hey, lil shit! You ready or what you fuckin' punk?"

"I kicked your ass once and I'll do again." As LT puts his fist up, he steps forward. He noticed that the whole school is out here to watch him fight. He also notices that Jake is scared, so LT takes one, two, three, quick steps, jumps up in the air, then came down hard on Jake's leg. A pop sound that everyone around heard came from the impact. As Jake falls to the ground screaming, crying out in pain, Bobby's boys grab Jake's crew and roughs them up a bit. Before Bobby and his boys leave LT steps up and tells him, "The next time, I'm gonna' break your arm and my boys are gonna' put your boys in the hospital with you."

"You broke my leg man. You broke my fuckin' leg!" is all Jake could say. As everybody left, nobody stepped up to help Jake or his boys. Needless to say, Jake would be out of school for a while, but his boys, they will be alright. LT got called down to the principal's office. The principal was very upset, but when he took one look at LT, he couldn't believe that this boy was the one responsible for breaking another boy's leg. The principal is shocked; especially that he did this to a boy that is so much bigger than he.

He told LT to sit down, "I will be with you in a minute." The principal followed upon the rest of his information calling down to the coach's office; he explained to the coach what took place this morning and demanded that he call Bobby and the rest of the boys up to his office immediately.

The coach, along with Bobby and the boys made their way through the doors that lead to the principal's office. The principal met them at the door calling them into his office. Now, standing straight up and mad as hell, he looked at Bobby and said, "Mr. Bobby Jones, the captain of our football team, you're gonna' tell me exactly what happened and who broke that boy's leg! Because one look at that little boy sitting out there and I know that he's not the one who did it."

"Mr. Simpson, sir, those boys, Jake, the one with broken leg and the rest of his friends were not only bullying and picking on Tim, but they beat him up yesterday before school. I know little Tim from my neighborhood, he hangs out with my little brother, so I wasn't going to let Jake or anyone put their hands on the little guy, too."

"So, you broke the kid's leg?"

"Sir. That's the funny thing; I did not break the kid's leg."

"So, if you did not, then who did, who did break his leg?"

"Tim did."

"I don't believe it."

"Maybe you should ask him for yourself, sir."

"Alright, coach Thomas; call that little boy in here."

"Young man, you need to get in here right now!"

"Okay."

"What's up, Bobby?"

"Hey, Tim."

"I didn't get you boys into any trouble, did I?"

"Don't worry about it, Tim. This is principal, Simpson."

"Young man, are you the one responsible for breaking that boy's leg?"

"Yes, sir!"

"I don't believe it!"

"Look, sir, he wanted to fight me so Bobby and his friends were there to make sure that

Jake and his friends wouldn't jump me like they did the last time."

"They beat you up before?"

"Yes, sir."

"Tell me one thing, Mr. Smiles. How did you break that kid's leg, he is so much bigger than you?"

"Well, I learned the move watching TV, sir; where you jump up and come down real hard on the knee."

"Wow! I really don't know what to say, but we'll have to suspend you. Whether you are being picked on, being bullied or not, it was you who bullied! I'm also going to have to talk to your parents."

"Both of my parents work the day shift, sir."

"Yeah, well I will tell your parents to call me as soon as possible, better yet, what is your telephone number? I will leave a message directly with your father. Mr. Sauce, I am highly disappointed in you, I can't believe you would allow something like that to happen. You are supposed to be a role model here at the school."

"There was nothing I could do about it, sir."

"Coach, I suspect there will be some type of discipline taken on our students?"

"Yes, sir."

"Good!"
"Mr. Smiles, you just have a seat right there until I get in touch with your parents."

Coach Liven whispered to Tim, "Don't worry about, Bobby." Then Tim heard him say to

Bobby out of earshot to the principal, "You did the right thing. You protected that boy. That's what leaders do! Alright, now we go on back to class and don't forget we got practices later.

"You say both your parents work during the day, huh? Unfortunately, we don't have a work number listed, so I have to send you home. But I will be sending a notice home to your parents and you better hope that li'l boy's parents don't press charges."

He spoke to some of his friends at school and they all think it should be good idea to form as a little neighborhood click to chase away all the bullies, or at least keep them from bullying others. Some of his friends live right around the corner. They met up at the basketball court every day so it would be nothing for them to click up every day. They all want to meet LT, who they've been hearing so much about. Well, as you know, LT was suspended from school. His parents got a phone call that same night from the principal and the next day they received a phone call from Jake's parents informing Mr. and Mrs. Smiles that they will be pressing charges against their son.

Needless to say, LT's parents end up paying hospital bills and LT finds himself in a little bit of court trouble. Over the next few years, LT and Billy form a click. As time goes by, they go from fighting to selling drugs, using drugs and drinking alcohol. Not too long, little Tim already lost his way, forgetting who he was. After a few years, Tim ended up in prison, while most of his friends got killed. This scenario was long and drawn out for two reasons; the first being this scenario was based from a true story with only a few things changed. The reason being was to show you that it does not matter where you live.

How you are raised and have family structure in your life doesn't matter if there is no communication, good constructive communication between the youth and the parents. If there is no lesson being taught to a child or young teen on how to deal with the type of pressures that young people go through, then they are left to their own devices, leading to irrational thinking. It is so easy to be victim to drugs, violence, and crime!

The violence he once feared, he embraced it. He engaged it. Now when he went down the street, no one messed with him. They loved him and respected him. Yes, because they like him. If he was that same man, they would pound his face in as they did before. It was the violence they respected and he knew it. He also knew that if he ever let down his guard, he would become a target again. So, he always carried a chip on his shoulders.

Tim liked spending most of his time with his little brothers and sisters, taking them for walks or to the park so they could play. He was always careful not to be violent or mean toward them. Never hitting or talking down to them. He was always teaching them or spoiling them more than anything. In the back of his mind, he wasn't too cool for his little brothers and sisters. He didn't mind spending time with them. He was also very protective of them. He doesn't want them to grow up the way he had grown up or at least develop the same attitude that he had.

At just 15 years old, he already felt like he was a man... a man who was always on the street corner. He had a lot of respect for his mother. She always made sure that there was dinner on the table. Through everything he watched her go through in life, she always maintained her integrity. He knew that she did the best she could with him like taking him to school, talking to his teachers in and out of appointments with doctors. She was always there for him. It wasn't her fault how he turned out. It was a decision he made and before she knew anything about it, it was too late.

The blood was already on his hands. She knew when she looked in his eyes at just 15 years old that he was already a man, so the relationship that they built was more so like brother and sister, than brother and mother and son. As time goes by, he actually does start turning into a young man. He starts dating all types of different women. And when I say women, I mean women. He went from dating strippers to prostitutes to regular girls holding a nine to five.

But as confident as he seemed, he always had problems with low self-esteem. The only thing he knew how to do was fight and sell drugs. He had a grade school education. He looked the part, but he didn't know much about anything but the streets. That was all good, when it came down to hood girls.
But the girls he craved for, weren't hood. He liked smart, intelligent women. At the age of 18, he started a job working at KFC. One day,

while working he met a woman. A woman who struck him so hard, he drops a bucket of chicken and made a mess... a mess of everything. The woman introduced him to a life he dreamed of since he was 10 years old. That's a normal life. A life he long forgot about.

CHAPTER 4

SO FAR, WE HAVE TALKED about fear, bullying, and control. We also identified the cause and effects of bullying, fear, and control. In this chapter, we are going to talk about low self-esteem. We are going to get into the story of this book. As I tell the story, I want you to see if you can notice how bullying, the name calling and all the boys went through as children plays an effect on his emotions, mentality and even his confidence.

I want you to recognize the low self-esteem and more so that triggers his faulty thinking. When we left off the boy was only 15. He quickly learned about street life. He became a part of a world that he never wanted to be a part of. For him, it just happens. The path was white. It was clear. There were no confusions.

Anyway, instead of confronting her again, knowing that they are just going to go back and forth. Also, knowing that she is just going to lie again, he attacked the situation with the same motivation he would use in the streets. But instead of anger, it is love that motivated him now, so he asked if she was worth it. Yes, she was. So now in his mind, it was a competition. To him she was just more than a prize. He also knew in his heart that he really did love her.

He felt that love would prevail and the only thing she did is underestimate him. Her not knowing who he really was. She knew his heart but she didn't know how he was connected. He knew people. A lot of the older guys in town really respected and liked him, so she found out a little bit of information on this dude. It turned out that this dude was more than just a football player. He was somewhat of a baller, hustling, selling drugs. Then he realized why her father disapproved of him and with that thought, he was left with a sour taste in his mouth for her father.

All he was thinking about, he asked himself, what was his position with his girl? Was he a rebound? And he shook out the thought that their relationship was much deeper than that. He concluded that she was cheating on the football player with him and vice-versa. She must have been unsure of the football player wannabe drug dealer. So, with that thought, he started working harder at his job and his relationship, putting in overtime on both, surprising his girl at work with flowers, showing up at her house just to say hi.

One day, he lost his job. At first, he didn't understand why because it wasn't his fault that he got hurt on the job. He was in the back, busting jugs, when he reached into the sink and cut his hand on a broken coffee pot. When the supervisor saw this, he was fired. He wrapped his hand up, grabbed his things and then left. Now, reading all the way to this point, it seems as if I am a pretty confident young man. The low self-esteem I suffer from as a child was working in the shadows of my mind. Remember that I said in the beginning of this chapter, I want you to see what triggers my low self-esteem, what triggers my faulty thinking and remember the whole point of this book is bullying and how it can affect you as an adult.

Now, what I am getting ready to tell you was hard for me to digest at that time. My girl has a younger sister. One day, the sister teased me or should I say picked at me about the way I stutter when I talk and not in a playful manner. She was being very mean, nasty, putting me down, and saying a lot of foul things. She was being very offending. This is the first time anyone has picked on me since

I turned 14 and this hurt me like a knife straight into my heart.

Why? Because I thought the sister was cool and my girl was standing right there. I was so stunned that I didn't know what to do. Me and the sister have a full blown argument right there. And I am so mad, hurt, and confused that I just walk away not wanting to embarrass myself any further. The sister accomplished what she wanted. It didn't take long for my girl to dump me and when I said dump me, I mean dump me.

Remember this is the same young man who was a little boy and told that he had attention deficit disorder. Learning disability and a speech and language problem, who got picked on and bullied on a regular basis, which was also dumped out of school in the ninth grade. But there is 'one' thing that he is really good at besides the negative attributes that I spoke of earlier, which is his discernment of people and who they are. He is really good at understanding people. But he truly never met another person like the woman that he is learning of now. Although he dropped out of school, he never lost his mind for learning. (Remember why he dropped out of school) With that being said, he loved to read and write poetry and philosophy.

But, let's get back to his relationship. This new woman he was dating now touched him in a way so hard that he started believing in a better life. He began believing in people again. She gave him hope to be himself, to be who he was. One day, while by himself, he cried so hard because of things he had done, all of the violence that he committed in his life. All of these years, he felt like he lost a part of himself that would never be found again and he found it in her. He found himself through her.

She gave him strength that he didn't even know. This young man was so happy that he stopped drinking, selling drugs, and even running the streets. All he wanted to do is work and spend time with his girl. Introducing to her his family, he wanted them all to be close. His brothers and sisters love her, but his mother really didn't like her. He felt like that would change over time though. Besides that, everything was running so smooth. They always went out on dates, or hung around the house.

They were always laughing, joking, and playing around with each other. And she felt so good with his lil' brothers and sisters and he loved that. But everything changed when she finally brought him home to meet her parents. As time goes by, he found out that from the beginning her father disapproved of his daughter being in any type of relationship with the young man. Somehow her father found out that he was a drug dealer, but what her father didn't know is that he stopped dealing drugs to be with his daughter. But all that doesn't matter now.

She was mad that she had to find this information about him from someone else, let alone her father of all people. When I told her about my past, I lied saying that I was just a regular guy who dropped out of school to help my mother with my little brothers and sisters. I was ashamed to tell the truth about why or what I went through. I didn't want her to look down on me. I was afraid that if I told her about school bullies, the choices I made, that she would judge me and I didn't want that.

I continued to work, trying to block everything out. I focused on doing everything I can to make my girl happy and everything seemed like it is going smooth. But one day, I found out that my girl was still seeing her ex-boyfriend who is a football player. I was crushed. I was hurt. I confronted her with this information. She denied it, looking me straight in my eyes, swearing that I am the only one. I believed her, never doubting her words. But as we keep hanging out together, going out together, meeting her friends and my friends. I keep hearing something about her. Now the young man might not have proper education but he wasn't a dummy. He was intelligent. Anyone could see that when you speak to him.

Remember all the conflicts, the hardships that he had endured. I mean, this wasn't your average kid that got picked on. Though the effects are the same for anyone getting bullied or abused, this kid had disabilities and he believed it to and he was weak then, but he is strong now.

Okay, back to my low self-esteem. What triggered this emotion in me? 1. The sister of the girl friend. 2. The Father showing his disapproval. The father disapproving of the relationship only made me work harder. So, it wasn't the father. It was the sister. She always had something mean and nasty to say. She reminded me of the teachers at school who used to punish me for sticking up and defending myself.

Now I was around her sister and she continued to be awful. That's not to say I didn't try. I did try my best to get to know the sister.

But she always made it clear that she didn't like me and that she mocked the way I stuttered, which really hurt. My girl, the woman who opened my eyes and gave me courage to be who I really am, dumped me. It broke my heart. It broke me. She was nothing like all the others. That low self-esteem was causing me to question myself in my mind again, as I did when I was a child. But this time, I was telling myself that it didn't matter what I did. I would always be a failure. I was just another punk kid who dropped out of high school. I was so scared to talk about my problems then and even more afraid to face those kids who used to bully me.

So, I decided that I would never be a good example for normal people. Let's face it; I got picked on for not being like the normal kids who used to put me down. I knew at just 16 years old that I was not normal, with all of the doctors, the teacher, and the bullies. So why am I trying to be normal anyway? This is what I told myself during the trip to South Carolina. It was a very long ride. It was a lot of time for me to drink. And with everything I thought of, I just accepted it for who I thought I was. I vowed to be an outlaw menace of society. I developed a hate for people that went way beyond the definition of what it means in the dictionary... on top of being patient to people always trying to taunt me.

Don't forget about what I went through in the streets. I developed an anti-social personality disorder. With that being said, I didn't care about a girlfriend just as much as I didn't care about missing friends. I wasn't going to allow another girl or person to break my heart again. But in the system of my heart, I just wanted to be so happy. All I ever wanted was to be happy. So, I got a puppy, and I treated that puppy better than I treated human being. Outside of my family, the puppy was my only friend.

Sometimes I wonder if dogs could talk, what would mine say. It was only a few months before my puppy died of parvo virus. I buried him in the ground thinking to myself, "This is how my life goes." What did I ever do to deserve so much pain? All I ever want was to be good kid.

I remember it clearly, telling my mother that I want to be a professor. Knowing full well that a professor is what I wanted to be, as instead I became a very insecure person relying on the drugs and alcohol to numb my pain. But drugs and alcohol just made my life worse. At the time, I didn't care though. I started feeling like an animal rather than a human being, wishing I could be just as carefree, learning about animals. Lions quickly became my favorite. Mimicking the behavior of a lion, I realized I became what I hate most in a bully.

She just left me sitting on the side of the curb. Literally, she just drove off. She came to me, asked if I wanted to go for a ride, and then said that we needed to talk. We got around the corner; she started talking about her father and her sister and just said we can't be together anymore. I told her to pull the car over. There's nothing else to talk about. Truth be told, I didn't know what the hell to say. She pulled the car over and I got out just sitting right there on the side of the curb. What hurt me the most, was that I was really trying to be a part of her life. When I do things, I don't do them half-way, I give my all. So, this really cut deep. I never felt so low in my life.

After this, I fell in a dark place. A place that was even darker than the first one, I went to when I was just a young teen, turning toward violence to protect myself from all of the bullying. But now I was broken by love, so what filled my heart was pain. I am going to back up right here just a little while. During the relationship with my girl, my family moves to South Carolina to be closer with the rest of the family down south. I remained behind because I was so in love with this girl.

But we split up. Now I am in Springfield alone, well not alone. I do know a lot of people, and I still have my aunts, uncles and cousins here. But there is nothing like having your mother when you need her and she and my mother are really close. I'm not a type of person to bother people with my problems. So, basically, I'm all alone. One night, I am so intoxicated that I fall asleep on someone else's porch. I really thought that I was at my place. Thank God that these people knew me.

I go through this bad spell for a week straight. Somehow, I find myself at my best friend's house. Don't ask me how, because I don't remember. What I do remember is my boy feeding me soup, well not feeding me soup, he made the soup. I ate, took a shower then went to sleep. I do remember I got into some problems with someone though I can't remember exactly who it was. When I woke up that next day my head was pounding and my boy wouldn't let me go anywhere by myself. As the days go by, my mother with all of my brothers pull up in front of the house and they jump out of the car like it was World War Three.

I mean, like literally, you should have seen their faces. My mother came running up to me, giving me hugs, making sure I was okay. I was so confused and puzzled to see all of their faces. I'm just like, "Yeah, ma. What are you guy's doing here?" Anyway, long story. They all convinced me to sit down with them, which don't take much convincing because I wanted to be close to my mother.

Now, all I want to do is talk about my low-self-esteem, so that you have a better understanding why I go from being confident and knowing what I want to falling into a pit of shame and sorrow.

Before you go any further, I recommend you go back to the beginning, reread the story... just the story, nothing else. See if you can see into my future. Remember, I asked you to assume, speculate, and draw conclusions. I also asked if the negativity I went through will carry over into adulthood and I said sure, it will.

Sure, he is still a young man, so in time, he will heal. But will he really heal from all of his wounds? Yes, he will, but I go through so much more before I do. It takes me a long time to really confront myself. I blamed a lot of people for so long that I forgot to look at the one most important person to me. I forget to look at the one person who needs me most, and that's me.

The only time I can remember anyone telling me that I could be someone in this world, was my mother. She is the only person I remember trying to be positive toward me. My mother is a great woman. Sometimes she would talk me about mean people, but I was just afraid to tell her what I was going through. I didn't want my mother to think that I was retarded, dumb or stupid. I didn't want my mother to think that I was soft. And I knew there were a million little kids out there just like me, which brings me to the poor tools of communication, teaching, learning, and knowing to use them correctly and effectively there will be boundaries set up around your child/children, your home, school friends, neighborhoods, etc.

These tools are sure ways to safeguard and protect your children/family as well as yourself. But more so than anything, I want to reach out to these kids out there. I want to encourage them and the teens, young, or even older adults, to step up against bullying, to speak up and tell their stories.

Don't be afraid or ashamed. We are all here for each other, those who are victims of bullying/abuse young or old, tell your story. Talk about your anger, reclaim your innocence. Together we can change things one step at a time. Even those kids will come to school ready to commit crime by taking the wrong way. Just like me, they have stories to tell.

So, tell it, I want you to tell them. Everybody needs to hear it. Tell the world that you are the real victim, even if it's all too late. I know that with me sitting in prison, people are not too keen on listening to me. But they will listen to you, to lend hands to push the bullies into a corner, back them down, push them aside and push them away.

CHAPTER 5

LOW SELF-ESTEEM STRIKES. You are always afraid to take a chance. You are the first one to put yourself down or come up with some lame excuse as to why you're good. I know because I've been there. All that second-guessing leaves one believing that there is someone better than oneself. So why even bother, right? Having low-self-esteem also left me with low self-confidence. I wanted to do things. I would think about having fun all the time. Doing things like skating or dancing, but those things aren't as fun if you're doing them alone. At least that's what I told myself, because I never really had friends and I wasn't the kind of guy who took chances.

But today, I know you don't need friends or other people to have fun and guess what, when you are having fun, other people will want to have fun with you. Just make sure they are good people. Not everyone who wants to get to know you is good for you, not everyone who wants to hang around you, are good people. They may seem good coming across as cool people but be careful. Some people are full of manipulation and evil. But all in all, just live your life.

Don't worry about others on what they do or what they think of you. Their thoughts about you make or break you, or control you. Some words might hurt you, but don't let them. I don't care if you are overweight, wear glasses, or have pimples. You have to find out what makes you who you are inside. What or who makes you happy. Don't worry about others who put you down, they're the ugly ones. If you don't have friends, look outside yourself and what you are good at, then do all you can to excel at that.

Whenever I look back at my life, it pains me to know that I became such a monster and my ex-girlfriend's sister wasn't the source of all of my insecurities and low self-esteem. It was all of the things I went through as a child that led me to that point. It was all of the bullying, abuse, picking, and name calling. It was the doctor's telling me about all the disabilities that I have that led me to believe that I wasn't good enough. It was the fear that kept me from talking to my mother. I didn't want her to think that there was something wrong with me too.

To this day, I never told my mother what I went through in school or even in the streets. I'm surprised now is as good as time as any, right? But I still have that fear in the back of mind of rejection that this is a hard one to get over. With as much as I have educated myself out of my incarceration, I still have that fear of rejection. But you would never know I struggled with disabilities unless I told you about it.

Today, I am working on preparation for my release and I see my life from a completely different perspective. My cup is half full now, for once, I can finally see that, but this is not the end of my story. There is more to come. Nor is this my full story. I am really just focusing on the aspects that are related or associated to the point of this book, so with that being said, let's get back to it, shall we?

This section of the book is about low self-esteem and how dangerous it is for anyone carrying its black cloud over their head. This feeling is like a disease, like a rotten apple to its core. It is only through our self-talk that we tell ourselves, "I will never be good enough. I will never be smart enough. I will never be handsome enough." You ever have those instances?

You can be your own worst enemy. I was mine. Yeah, some of those older kids bullied, picked on me, put me down, and called me all kinds of names. But I believed it was because I didn't believe in myself. I had no self-worth. I defeated myself with it, and put myself down.

I'm sure everything I went through played a part in why I had chosen the path I traveled. But I chose to become nothing but a failure sitting behind doors. Nobody chose that but me. Another expression comes to my mind. Watch your actions because they become your words. Watch your words because they become your thoughts or watch your thoughts because these become your words. Watch your words because they become your actions, so with that being said, watch your actions because your actions affect other people.

Well, this statement is so true. There is something else that comes to my mind. I hear people say all the words don't mean a thing, sticks and stones may break my bones but words will never break me. Well, I just want to see the person who came up with this noisy rhythm. Words have meaning and the choice of words that you use to express yourself will be the cause and effect of another person's direction. Words can build but still destroy or even start a riot. If I tell you you're ugly, you're fat, you're stupid, that you will never be anything, that does have impact on other you.

You would be hurt. You may even question yourself as an adult. If I lean toward you and say, "Fuck you!" you are going to be mad. This is why, I don't respect people who play with their words. You take a bully at its value. For example, if I tell you I love you when I do not, in time, it will show and then this takes away the value of the word. This is about the reason for people saying that words don't mean anything. This is also the reason for the noisy rhyme. To protect you as a child from those mean and noisy words that other children like to use as a means to put you down.

So, you should:

1. Surround yourself with good, positive people.
2. Engage in positive activities.
3. Do things that will uplift you mentally.
4. Do things that you like to do and find somebody whom you can share those thoughts with. That was my problem. I don't make friends.

I didn't have any friends, so I had no support. You need to build a good support team. People you depend on and rely on when you are going through things. It's all about building good structure in your life, so you won't have to go out alone and don't forget about good positive self-talk.

To defeat low self-esteem, is to defeat every person that put you down in your life, and defeat every single negative thought that you have of yourself. To defeat low self-esteem is to free your mind, to free your mind is to free yourself from all of the shame, from all of the guilt. You must let it all go. How? By looking in the mirror and telling yourself who you are. Not what they say you are, but who you are deep down in your soul as a human being.

You have to find the good qualities in you, that beautiful person that lies within yourself, inside of your mind because that's who you are. Remember, people put you down to make themselves feel more in control and powerful. If someone calls me a thief and I am not a thief, then what does it matter? If someone calls me a liar and I am not a liar, then what does it matter? But it does matter. It's the intent that matters. It's the assault that matters. It's the put down that matters. It's the hurt, the feeling, and the pain that matters. It's the feeling of not being accepted that matters, but only if you let it matter. So be strong, hold your head up high, and let your mind fly.

Words are very powerful when expressed through emotions. Young adults and young teens do not realize what type of effects their words or actions will have on others. With words, one can build you or break you down. For instance, if a father tells his son, "Come on big guy!" "You're really smart buddy!" or "Champ, what you are doing?" These are all words of encouragement, building up confidence, and boosting self-esteem.

The same goes for children, young ones and young adults. If a 12-year-old tells a kid, "You're ugly, fat, and stupid, I don't like you!" Wow! What a hard show, but if that same 12-year-old says, "You are really smart. You are a really cool person. Wow! Wow, that's awesome!" Just that little statement right there is so empowering. That's the thing for me; encouragement is a really big deal. The more we encourage each other, to be better, to do better, the more we help each other, the way it brings positivity into our homes, and in turn will spread into our neighborhoods, schools and ultimately into the world.

Low self-esteem was a really ugly reflection of me in my life. And I say my life, because that's how I was functioning at the time. Anyone close to me knows that I was struggling with the negative attitudes and insecurities held within myself. I brainwashed myself into believing that's who I was, convinced that I would never amount to nothing.

Depression was like an evil monster that fed on my low self-esteem. It's evil twin that I had to battle against, for a very long time. All the way up until my conviction. It was in prison that I finally defeated these two goons that were robbing me of a healthy lifestyle. When

I realized that it was all in my head, that it was my own negative stinking thinking, then it became easy for me the correct myself. It became easy for me to let go of everything. Today, I can honestly say that the ugly things that put me down, made it possible to now find myself.

You have good qualities about you. You can make friends. You just have to make friends that believe like you, who share the same interest with common goals, who share the same dreams. I am going to tell you how I get over my low self-esteem and it wasn't that hard either. One day, I woke up and I started really thinking about me, about who I am as a person, a human being. And I realized that I have a good heart. I am a good person. I always try to help people.

If you are broken down on the side of the road, I will stop to help you and I don't like to see people hungry, hurting, or in pain. I looked in the mirror, passed all of the bullying and name calling. All of the doctors, all of my so-called disabilities, all of the teachers, all of the people that ever put me down, all of the negative things that I've done.

I looked passed the man in the mirror and I said, "I am better than that." I told myself that I am better than all of those people. I am smart. I am beautiful. I am handsome. I am intelligent. There is nothing wrong with me. There are people messed up, but not me. There are people that missed out on a good friend, but not me. Those people are the monsters, not me!

Instantly, I started to feel better about myself. Through positive self-talk, I started bullying courage. I started gaining confidence. Why? It's because I believe in it. I believe what I was telling myself. I started learning more about me. And you know what? Sitting here in this empty cell, I found that lost little boy deep down inside of my heart. Hiding in the darkness and my soul, and I cried. I cried out of fear. I cried out of joy. I cried because I found myself and today it is that little guy who speaks from his heart. I am alive and I am ready to live my life free of pain, free of shame, free of guilt. I have suffered long enough.

It is time for me to be free and the only way I can do that is to let it all go. I am not a failure. I am just myself. I am going to live for today. I am going to work today to live because tomorrow is a better day - Living through these transitions in my life, living this wonderful miracle... a changing of my mind. I drank from a cup that was completely empty. I didn't care about making my tomorrow a better day, because I didn't believe in better ones. I didn't believe in a better life. I didn't believe in humanity. But today, I drank from a cup that is full. I feel like I have a new chance at life. I am sitting here in prison and I feel like I have a new chance at life.

I am sitting here in prison and I feel like I am a new man and I still have 10 years left and it's not because of church or religion because I can't go to church, but it is because of God. You have to want something so bad to believe it just applies. I was tired of my life, so tired of myself. I was so tired of just living.

I used to pray to God all the time and I still pray to God all the time. You can call me weak but only a person with a strong heart can live through what I have gone through from the start.

This book is only a small portion of my life. I am only wanting to focus on bullying from a victim's stand point. To show you the behavioral disorders of a victim. Now I know my story is different. But that's the unique thing. We all have different stories, but the pain is the same? The hurt is the same. The experience is the same and anyone who has been a victim of bullying or abuse knows that pain. Knows how it hurts. Knows how it feels. You can relate because you have been there.

Juggling the same questions, I have. Am I a failure? Am I really stupid? Am I really ugly?

No, you're not! You are a beautiful, intelligent, sophisticated human being, full of wonders and miracles, curiosity and life, so don't let anyone put you down or put out your light. Only you hold the power to do that, no one else! You ever hear the expression, birds of a feather, flock together? Well, this is all so true. You can be a good-hearted person but will become like those of your surroundings.

But before this is where I wanted to change. I would force myself not to care about my heart and how I feel. I would force myself not to believe or force anyone through negative self-talks. I would tell myself that I am all that I need. And for anyone of you reading this, if you ever had a broken heart, you know after leaving, you gave your all, sharing with them who you are, and all of your secrets.

There are things that would even shame your mother. You know it is hard for you to give it all again, because you fall into things that you can't stop, like bullying, violence, drugs, and alcohol. And what do you get?

I became a monster, that left me not caring whether people liked me or not. Those close to me knew if they were special to me, because if someone other than them even said something I felt was wrong, I wouldn't hurt them anymore. No one ever cared about me, so why should I care about anyone else?

I'd started seeing the world through a small lens. Drinking and getting high every day. I remember wanting to die, because I was so miserable. My heart was filled with so much pain. Sometimes, I would go around, picking fights, hoping to be taken out of this life. I remember this one guy put a gun to my head. I told him to pull the trigger. I even started fighting with him, hoping he would shoot. I could feel the tears welling up in my eyes as I sit here and write to you thinking about how I used to be when all I ever wanted to be was a good child. I had so many hopes and dreams.

I blamed so many people for so many years when I was the one who messed myself of my innocence and now, I am sitting in prison doing a long sentence. I've been in since 2006 with a release date of 2024, but hopefully that will change. I can honestly say, with these tears in my eyes, thinking of all regrets and bad choices I made, I truly thank God, because I have never been so free. It doesn't make any sense to me because I am not supposed to be free. I am not supposed to be happy.

Prison is an institute that breeds raw hate. Walking around with a smile on my face goes against the grain. Sometimes I have to hide my joy, depending on what area of the prison I am in. Sometimes I don't understand why I am so happy. I just woke up one day and I've been that way ever since, and now I think about that little boy or girl out there who is just like me, being forced into a life that is filled with so much pain. In some of us, bullying is just the first monster that we have to face.

I want to make it so bullying is a monster that no one will ever have to face again.

The reason is because I knew it. Bullying forced me into a life of violence. It will do it to the next child out there who thinks just like me. The only way to make it stop is to make it stop.

So, that we will never again see a beautiful little girl or handsome young man take their own life, all because of bullies and for those adults who mistreated children, who mistreat their students. How dare you lose the trust of an innocent, pure little child! How dare you force your strength on a child? How dare you to take advantage of our most precious human beings... leaving them ashamed of themselves. The time is now for American citizens to march in unity against these bullies.

March against the schools. March against the neighborhoods, the communities. Join hands and protest with integrity, with courage, with strength, with love, with the power of coming together. For me, it's doing more than implementing a law. A law doesn't stop a criminal from committing a crime. So how is a law going to stop a bully from being mean or slamming your kid's head into a locker?

I use this experience as a stepping stone and I am truly grateful for this experience, because it helped me find myself. I found my heart. I found my strength. I didn't know I could be so strong. I didn't know how strong I was until that day I was sitting at my cell all alone crying. My heart used to be so sad and so heavy. I never realized how rotten I was inside until that day.

Ever since that day, I wake up feeling brand new, ready to take on the world. I wake up every day looking and seeing all of the possibilities, all of the opportunities to make my life better, to make myself better and I want so desperately to help this young generation of hope, peace, love, happiness, opportunity, courage strength and inspiration to change to live, to breathe easy, to be free of a mental prison to live a life, breaking all barriers because you can't live a life free with no limits.

It's tough dealing with insecurities, low self-esteem, fear, shame, guilt, or any other grappling attitudes or behaviors.
Now, let's get into mystery. I go lower before I go higher. Living in South Carolina was

crazy! After about a year, I moved back to Moss.

Once I saw my ex and she came running up to me, literally running to me, squeezing me, telling how much she missed me, that she loves me and she should have never left me. I didn't know what to say. I was at a loss for words. Here was a person who hurt me, literally drove away, leaving me sitting on the curb, and now she is, after a couple of years, kissing me and telling me how much she missed me. Of course, I hugged her back, asking her how she is doing. She gave me her number, and told me I should give her a call anytime. So, I did. Real affection is something I went without throughout the time we were split.

But she wanted a relationship more than just some affection, and to be honest, I wanted the same. She apologized to me hundreds of times in many ways and I believed her. Maybe I wanted to believe her because she gave me confidence and I felt like a real man when I was with her. You got to remember, this is the same girl who broke through my ice, cold heart at just the tender age of 18, who came into my life when I didn't have faith and trust in human beings. But she ultimately broke my heart again, proving me wrong and put her in that category of human beings. But at the time, she made me feel like I had self-worth.

She made me feel like I was a human being. When we were together, it felt like it was just her and, but I was the fool and thought I was in paradise. This is the real world. After our first break up, I became really wild. I had my insecurities, low self-esteem, and fears. I didn't care about my feelings. I would block them. I was numb to the world around me, not because of her but because of everything I went through.

I thought she was just the person that trusted me, purely. I had become 10 times worse than when I was a teen. I didn't care about anybody and everything was all about me. I became reckless, a person manipulating everyone around me for my own personal gain. I wouldn't let anyone close to me. My mentality was so bad that I had to stop thinking of my own family. I didn't want to be around them like that.

I honestly never did anything to hurt her. I didn't trust her. I didn't trust anyone, and I didn't want to. I wasn't going to let anyone physically, mentally, or emotionally be close to me. But slowly, she was phasing in, and every time I felt like she was getting too close, I would push her away until one day I finally broke down to her telling her about my bad habits, about my low self-esteem, sharing with her about some of the things I went through in my life and some of the things I did. I told her I wanted to change, but this time I wanted to change for me. I didn't want to be a monster anymore. I just wanted to be happy.

I stopped selling drugs, drinking, and getting high. I got a real job working construction, I became a working man and I started feeling good about myself. I started thinking outside of the box and meeting new people. I started going to church and I even started helping the kids in the neighborhood, providing a safe environment for them. I felt like I had a good girl and I was going to lose her to my own selfish ways, so I bought a diamond ring. I did it big. I got down on my knee and asked her to marry me and she accepted. In my heart, I wanted to give her the world. But like I said, I was the fool.

CHAPTER 6

WELCOME TO THE TRUTH behind the scenes. In this chapter, you are going to hear from real criminals and prisoners sentenced to do hard time as inmates inside our country's federal penitentiary system. These are their stories. Let me just say, before we hear from these inmates, that I came up with a questionnaire consisting of 9 specific questions. I conducted these interviews right out of my very own cell. For security reasons,

I cannot say or state what cell number or unit that is. Some of these individuals wish to remain anonymous, but all of them want their voice to be heard. So, let's get to it. My questions and replies will be in BOLD font to better help you clarify who is speaking.

Our first interview is with Mr. Travis III:

Hello, Mr. Travis III. How are you doing today?

I am doing fine, thank you!

Before we begin, let me just say that I really appreciate you volunteering your time. I know you are a busy man and there are other things you can be doing with your time. So, thank you for sitting down here with me today!

I am obliged, Mr. Savageau, to be a part of this book and I thank you for providing me with the opportunity.

Let me just say, Mr. Travis, that I am looking for that raw sincerity... that raw deep feeling and emotion. As I ask you these questions, I want you to go back to that place when you were just a sweet innocent little child. Are you ready?

Yes, sir.

Okay, here we go. First question: Were you a victim of bullying as a young child or young teen?

Yes, as a young teen.

Man, that's tough. What can you tell me about your experiences of bullying and the effects of how bullying made you feel?

I started suppressing anger early, which leads to violent outburst and attacks. Finally, it got to the point where I couldn't take it anymore.

Wow, that's really something man, that's really something. Okay, do you still suffer from the effects of bullying today as an adult, such as people putting you down, hurting you, or any other type of paranoia or distrust in people because of the bullying you suffered from as a child? If yes, how does this make you feel?

No, because I stopped taking crap from people.

Okay, that's good. Do you think or believe bullying has a direct link or cause for becoming a criminal?

For some individuals, yes. I know that it does.

Alright moving right along... Do you think or believe that victims of bullying become violent outcast criminals of society?

Again, yes. But there are victims that don't become violent toward society but violent towards themselves because of low self-esteem.

Please elaborate in your own words, utilizing your own experiences of your life, explaining the connection between bullying and a criminal lifestyle?

For me, and the situation that I was in, I had the dilemma of retaliating and getting kicked out of school or dealing with it and continue to get good grades.

All the while, I developed a deep hatred toward bullies and made a promise to myself that one day I would repay the bullies and give them all hell. I decided any business operation or person that had a lot of money must be robbed as I was robbed of my peace and space by the bullies.

Wow! That's really deep, man. Can you please explain the effects and problems that you experienced as a child or young teen such as a frustration, and not being able at communicating with your peers, adults, or your parents?

The frustration and distress came from whoever you confide in about the bullying, telling you, everyone goes through that in school or deals with it in life. Making it a small issue or hearing if you kick their ass, they'll leave you alone. But then it happens, and I do kick their ass, then get suspended from school or go to jail and afterwards receive a home ass whipping or verbal threating for getting in trouble.

So, it's like a no-win situation either way, which leads to a person not saying anything at all. Because they don't want to tell or get in trouble, which is a big reason why these mass school shootings take place or young kids are caught with hand guns at school. They have no one to turn to. They turn to themselves for the answer to stop being pushed around or made fun of.

Wow, I couldn't agree with you more, Mr. Travis. Can you explain the behaviors or attitude that you develop as a direct cause of the bullying experiences in your life as a young youth?

Once I had enough, I decided that anyone who cracked on me or tried to harass me or punk me had 14 days before I enacted revenge in some way to them or their family, which wasn't good because I was young, thinking this way. Music is what saved a lot of people from funerals.

Wow! That was good. I appreciate your honesty right here. Now we come to our last question, you ready?

Yes, sir.

Okay, here we go. After answering questions 1 through 8, is there anything else you would like to share with the readers and myself regarding bullying or maybe something you would want them to know concerning your views about bullying on our young youth of today?

First, there is a difference between jeering with peers and harassment and bullying. These days, when a 6th grader feels he has to bring a gun to school to keep someone off him, that means the adults in his life are slipping all around the board. From the parents to the teachers, be more than aware, be watchful.

Thank you, Mr. Travis, I really appreciate your participation. I really appreciate your opening up to me on such a deep level. It really means a lot to me. The people of our country really need to hear our stories. I feel like the more people we get to speak up and speak out against bullying, the impact will be that much greater... especially coming from us, as prisoners. I believe our stories will bring an entirely different light to the issue of bullying. What do you think?

Well, as I expressed to you before, Mr. Savageau, I think what you are doing, writing this book, as well as including your story within it, is something really special. It's definitely going to open up the eyes of America, and being that we are federal inmates; it is definitely going to open the eyes of the people who think that bullying is something not to be taken lightly, so thank you, I really appreciate it.

Well thank you, Mr. Travis. I really appreciate you. It really means a lot to me. So, thank you.

So, America, as you can see, bullying affects everyone. Some of us in here, no, a lot of us in here, were once sweet, innocent little children, just looking to find our way but somewhere along the road, while trying to find our way, made a wrong turn. Dealing with the frustrations and pressures of a world we weren't prepared for. And this is my wish – to create a more conscious, more aware people, who won't think bullying is just a normal part of everyday life.

Although it is a part of our everyday lives, it is not normal, nor should it be acceptable. So, we need to start teaching our young ones how to deal with all of the social pressures that come about the territory of a society that is so divided against each other. Let's move along to our next interview. Shall we?

Good morning T. How are you doing this morning?

I'm good.

That's great. Let me just say, before we get started, that I really appreciate your participation. I appreciate you volunteering your time here this morning. It really means a lot to me to have you and the rest of the guys step up and be part of this story. Were you a victim of bullying as a young child or young teen?

Yes.

What can you tell me about your experiences of bullying and the effects of how bullying made you feel?

Getting beat up, getting my shoes taken, and made fun of... It all affected my self-esteem. I allowed people to put me down so much that I gave up on myself, that I didn't accomplish goals that I set for myself.

Man, I don't even know what to say but I appreciate your honesty. We're going to be a great interview. Man, I salute you.

Because it takes a lot of courage to sit here and even share that with someone and the fact that you're sharing this with me means a lot to me. So, I thank you Bro! Thank you for sitting here with me this morning.

It's not a problem. I am actually inspired by you. When you are talking in front of the community?

Well, thank you T. Thank you. You inspire me bro, guys like you inspire me. You ready for our next question?

Yeah.

Okay, do you still suffer from the effects of bullying today as an adult, such as people putting you down, hurting you, or any other type of paranoia or distrust in people because of the bullying you suffered from as a child? If yes, how does this make you feel?

Yes, I do. It makes me feel alone, angry doubting myself. I have been put down so much in the past. When someone tries to help me, I don't open up because I feel like they will use that against me. Because of my experiences of bullying, it is hard for me to trust people.

I really appreciate you opening up like this to me. I really do. It's going to be really good for this book, so thank you! Thank you! Do you think or believe bullying has a direct link or cause for becoming a criminal?

Yes.

Do you think or believe that victims of bullying become violent outcast criminals of society?

Yes.

Please elaborate in your own words, utilizing your own experiences of your life, explaining the connection between bullying and a criminal lifestyle?

When I was bullied, it made me feel alone. So, I looked up to negative influences. It was so much anger built up in me from being bullied. I couldn't take it anymore. So, I would act and do the same things that people would do to me.

Man, your story is going to encourage a lot of people. A lot of people! Can you please explain the effects and problems that you experienced as a child or young teen such as a frustration, and not being able at communicating with your peers, adults, or your parents?

When I was being bullied at school, I kept it in, no one knew I was being bullied. Everyone thought that everything was alright. But really on the inside, everything was all bad. I thought people would look at me different, look at me as weak... because I didn't defend myself. I put in my head that everyone was out to get me. I felt embarrassed to talk to my mother or my father.

Can you explain the behaviors or attitude that you develop as a direct cause of the bullying experiences in your life as a young youth?

Fighting and smoking weed. I started fighting because of the anger built from being bullied. I got tired of people picking on me. I started smoking weed because it took my mind off of the bullying. I started because, basically, it took my mind off of everything that was happening.

After answering questions 1 through 8, is there anything else you would like to share with the readers and myself regarding bullying or maybe something you would want them to know concerning your views about bullying on our young youth of today?

Don't hold it in. Talk to someone about it. Don't let it affect you like most people do.

Well, that completes our interview. But before you leave, I want to tell you that you're a brave man and I encourage you to never give up on yourself especially at someone else's expense. You have your entire life ahead of you and you can do some great things. You're very intelligent, so take this time out of your life and learn as much as you possibly can. Read as many books as you can. You did the right thing by coming to this program continue to stay on this path. Thank you, Tito!

No, thank you and have a great day.

Now, to you the reader! Can you see the similarities in the behaviors of even one of these gentlemen that I have just interviewed? How they ultimately turn toward violence? Like I said, the effect is the same on everyone. Keep that in mind as you read through these last three interviews. Then you tell me what all of these men have in common! Let's proceed to our next interview.

Good morning Mr. Mack! How are you doing this morning?

I am doing fine thank you.

Great. Before we get started, I would just like to say I really appreciate you participating here this morning. I really appreciate you stepping up like this. We all have a story and America really needs to hear yours. I feel like the more people we get to speak up and speak out against bullying, will make that much more of a difference, so thank you. It really means a lot to me.

Well, you inspire me, Mr. Savageau. What you are doing is really great. The time is now for you to put your story out there. I believe the book is going to be really big. When I heard you talking the other day, you inspired me. The way you were going around the unit pulling guys up. You are going to do some great things in your life, Mr. Savageau.

Thank you, Mr. Mack. I really appreciate that. You ready for our first question?

Yes, Sir!

Oh! Before we get started, I am looking for the raw deep emotion. I am looking for sincerity. I am looking for truth. I want you to go back to that place when you were a child. When you were just a young teen and bring that experience to the table. You ready?

Yes, Sir!

Were you a victim of bullying as a young child or young teen?

Yes. As a young child when I was between 7-12 years old.

Wow. That must have been really hard for you. What can you tell me about your experiences of bullying and the effects of how bullying made you feel?

It was an extremely difficult time for me. It caused me to have extremely low self-esteem then and even today as an adult, I suffer from, some of the effects.

Man, that's exactly what I am looking for, that truth right there. This is really going to be a really great interview! Okay, do you still suffer from the effects of bullying today as an adult, such as people putting you down, hurting you, or any other type of paranoia or distrust in people because of the bullying you suffered from as a child?

I felt fear and confusion. I didn't understand what made me target at the time or why it was happening to me.

Wow! That's something man. That's something. Do you think or believe bullying has a direct link or cause for becoming a criminal?

Yes, I avoid concentration in my relationships and sometimes I view constructive criticism as being put down by others and often I'm passive aggressive.

I really appreciate your opening up like this. Do you think or believe that victims of bullying become violent outcast criminals of society?

Yes.

Okay. Please elaborate in your own words, utilizing your own experiences of your life, explaining the connection between bullying and a criminal lifestyle?

Self-esteem gets over or under compensated. Some individuals stay victims all of their life. I over compensated and as a result for a long period of time in my life I became what I despised, a bully!

I appreciate your honesty Mack. It's going to be a great for this book. That really means a lot to me. Can you please explain the effects and problems that you experienced as a child or young teen such as a frustration, and not being able at communicating with your peers, adults, or your parents?

I suffered the emotions that I experienced. My mother was a single parent of three. She often wasn't available for me to talk to. When she was, I thought if I told her she wouldn't understand. I would seem weak or it would cause her more trouble or stress.

What you are saying right now is so, so, real. Children look up to their parents. They avoid certain conversations because they do not want to appear weak and at the same time they want to be accepted not rejected.

So, that was a very good statement you just made, Mr. Mack! Okay, moving right along. Can you explain the behaviors or attitude that you develop as a direct cause of the bullying experiences in your life as a young youth?

As I grew older, I noticed that responding with violence and aggression stopped the bullying. It made me feel powerful and in control. Not wanting to give up this feeling, I practiced this technique more.

That is a really deep statement right there, bro. Everything you are telling about is exactly what I am looking for. This interview is definitely going to be one of the top five featured in my book. Let's move on to our last question! After answering questions 1 through 8, is there anything else you would like to share with the readers and myself regarding bullying or maybe something you would want them to know concerning your views about bullying on our young youth of today?

I think the campaign against bullying is long overdue. As children, I think that a lack of understanding as well as other factors stimulates bullies. I feel sorry for bullies; they are sick people, just as I was when I practiced bullying. I got my self-worth and values from putting others down. When the truth is, this is the source of real values, and is worth more than the individual who has no values and is worthless. They are a burden instead of a blessing to others.

I couldn't agree with you more, Mr. Mack. That is the thing for me. For those of us who fell victim to their worthlessness, who fell victim you more Mr. Mack and this is the timing for me. Who knows, what it is like to, to have experienced this, this disease is cause for a mental stagnation. It is on us to step up. It is on us to make a stand. It is on us to tell our stories and this is the purpose of this book. That is the purpose of me and you telling our stories to show America that bullying is a psychological issue that really needs strict attention! Mr. Mack, you have been a blessing here today. Thank you for your time and attendance. it is most appreciated.

Thank you, Mr. Savageau.

Okay ladies and gentlemen, this is our fourth interview, and as you can see the end result is the same; violence. Keep in mind how the effects of the bullying stay locked, trapped deep inside of their minds. I hope that by the time you are done reading this that you can see and recognize how the behavioral disorders, social disorders and even mental disorders stay with you. Even as an adult and I say with you because this can possibly be you!

Moving on to our next interview... Good morning Mr. Rudd. How are you doing this morning?

I'm good and yourself?

I'm doing great this morning. Thank you for asking! Well, before we get started let me just say I really appreciate your participation here this morning. Thank you for your time. It really means a lot to me.

You inspire me, Bro!

You know everybody keeps saying that, Rudd.

That's because that's true. Bro. You inspire a lot of the guys around here. Ever since I started this program, everybody always has something good to say about you. I knew from the first time that I met you that you were a good dude! You don't meet a lot of dudes like you in prison. As a matter of fact, you don't meet dudes like you at all in prison.

Wow! That's a real big compliment! I really appreciate that you said that.

No. It's true, Man. Ask anyone of the guys around here, they all say the same thing.

Wow, that's truly amazing man. That really means a lot to me. I really don't know what to say...but thank you man. Thank you. You ready to get started?

Yeah sure, whenever you're ready.

Were you a victim of bullying as a young child or young teen?

Yes, since the 6th grade.

Wow, the 6th grade? What can you tell me about your experiences of bullying and the effects of how bullying made you feel?

In the 6th grade, at the school, as an 8th grader threw spit balls at me, and hit me in the rib on the walkway. I stabbed him in the face with a pencil. His friend helped me and the bus driver broke it up by seating us front to back. I invited him to see me at my house. A week later they both showed up and my twin brother and I abused them.

Wow! That was some experience you went through! Okay, do you still suffer from the effects of bullying today as an adult, such as people putting you down, hurting you, or any other type of paranoia or distrust in people because of the bullying you suffered from as a child?

Why is he doing this to me? I didn't do anything to him! Feelings of anger.
Do you think or believe bullying has a direct link or cause for becoming a criminal?

No!

Do you think or believe that victims of bullying become violent outcast criminals of society?

Hell, yeah! Yeah! I think that resentment from bullying is a build-up leading to a criminal lifestyle.

That was a great answer. I like that answer. Please elaborate in your own words, utilizing your own experiences of your life, explaining the connection between bullying and a criminal lifestyle?

Yeah. Pretty much stems from prior question which causes one to respond violently and aggressively.

Please elaborate in your own words, utilizing your own experiences of your life, explaining the connection between bullying and a criminal lifestyle?

It's almost like you begin rebelling against the law or any type of authority because you feel as though bullying is infringing upon you and you begin responding by instantly associating with feelings of rage and violence.

I like that word you just used, infringing. This is very true. Bullying is forced upon us!

And what you just said is exactly what I am looking for. How a victim of bullying rebels against any type of authority. Okay, the next questin. Can you please explain the effects and problems that you experienced as a child or young teen such as a frustration, and not being able at communicating with yur peers, adults, or your parents?

This differs for me because this is an agitation to me. Because there's a generation gap, it's an agitation not an emotional response; I think the frustration comes from the limited response expected by adult figures. I had issues of craving violence to fill a void of emotions that I didn't understand why I couldn't hurt people to fill this void.

Wow! That's going to make a great addition to this book, Mr. Rudd. I appreciate you being so open with me for this books. Raw and uncut is exactly what I want to give the people reading this book.

Can you explain the behaviors or attitude that you developed as a direct cause of the bullying experiences in your life as a young youth?

I believe it caused me to develop an attitude that is absolutely necessary to respond with as much as possible to someone who means me or means harm.

Okay, that is good. That is really good. You know everything you said here is along the lines of this book, which is great, absolutely great! Alright, last question. After answering questions 1 through 8, is there anything else you would like to share with the readers and myself regarding bullying or maybe something you would want them to know concerning your views about bullying on our young youth of today?

Bullying has a direct affect and or link on how an experience can present adversity to our own psychological make up. That goes beyond somethings that can be experienced in words. Other people need to step in and take a greater stance of interest and involvement with what's going on. I once saw a girl in the 6th grade getting pushed around on the lockers by several females and two boys. I intervened with violence; I was already a victim of bullying turning toward a violent lifestyle.

So, you see ladies and gentlemen, bullying does have a major effect on your young minds. I hope that these men who have just shared their stories with you had a major impact on you. Like I said in the beginning, you may not agree with it all, but by the time you are done reading this book, you will feel the full weight and impact of these stories. Including mine. This is your proof. Whether you believe me or not, the proof is in the book.

Let's continue to read. Now, before we move on, I ran across a guy, he was a late interview. I had to interview him myself personally, without my stenographer, and I am glad that I did. This interview was very deep for me. Now, I did my best to recall every word that was spoken between us during this interview, although I did leave certain pieces of our conversation out.

Some things are better left alone. Initially, I only chose 5 interviews to be in the main body of this book... but this young man touched my heart in a way that can I not even express with words.

The entire session with this young man was very moving. I walked away from this interview feeling a heavy weight on my chest, and to this day I continue to talk constructively with this young man. This young man is very special individual. It was only right for me to include his story in this book.

The interview should touch you deeper than any one of these stories. Although these are all great stories, this one means the most to me. So, with that being said, let me introduce you to Mr. Vladimir.

Mr. Vladimir, please come in, sit down. Thanks for coming. Thank you for showing up, this really means a lot to me.

Thank you. I remember you were talking about writing a book about bullying. You said you were writing your story in the book. I remember you was passing out these papers with these questions and you were trying to encourage guys to tell their story. Then I saw you this morning grabbing guys and pulling them into your cell. I figured you must be doing the interviews about your book, so I came over here.

And I am glad you did, Mr. Vladimir. I had to go around and start grabbing guys because no one was turning their questionnaires and this was holding me up, so with these questionnaires being a vital piece of my book with the help of one of the guys we decided to conduct interviews right out of my cell. I was really liking it.

But you are going to have to bear with me because Alley, who is my stenographer, is cut on a call out, so it is going to be just me and you. Before we get started, let me just say that I am looking for that raw truth, that raw pure sincerity. I want you to go back to that time when you were just a child. I want you to bring that emotion, that deep, felt emotion that experience to the table.

I want you to relive that time, relive that experience and bring that to this book and I guarantee you through the power of words and through the power of our stories, we will reach the minds and the ears of those who really need to hear what we have to say! Are you ready?

Yes, Sir!

Okay, here we go. Were you a victim of bullying as a young child or young teen?

Both as young child and teen.

Wow! That's hard man. That's hard. What can you tell me about your experiences of bullying and the effects of how bullying made you feel?

Deep! It started as a child with my stepfather. At four-years-old, my younger brother was born. My stepfather showed me that I would have to battle for attention. To him, I was no longer his son and it was very hurtful for me. By the time I was 8 years old, I was coming away, in and out of social services dealing with physical and mental abuse. Most of the time, sharing my life with others is out of the question because the abuse me and my mother suffered, isn't something I like sharing.

Vladimir, I want to shake your hand. You are a very strong young man to sit down here and even talk to me about this. It takes a lot of courage and I'm really touched and greatly and deeply honored that you even see me as someone you can talk to. It means a great big deal to be able to talk to someone like you. You are very intelligent and very brave! So, thank you.

The pleasure is mine.

Are you ready for the next question? Yeah.

Okay, do you still suffer from the effects of bullying today as an adult, such as people putting you down, hurting you, or any other type of paranoia or distrust in people because of the bullying you suffered from as a child?

Bullying is not cool. I've been bullied by my stepfather. My mother always took his side. So, I was alone and always searching for affection. Lucky for me! I had my mother's friends there to comfort me! But the basic functioning, I needed to grow was something I never knew. I've been bullied at school by bullies causing low self-esteem.

I was a follower which lead me to prison. Never saying no, I was used and taken advantage of.

Man, that is so deep right there. There are so many young adults as well as adults who are afraid to say what you just said. There are so many people who need to hear what you have to say. Your story is going to inspire so many people. Vlad, this is going to be really great for the both of us. Man, this is going to be so good! Do you think or believe bullying has a direct link or cause for becoming a criminal?

Nowadays, I don't suffer because I understand bullying as well as myself. I utilize fundamental principles. I can now say no and own my own place in life.

Wow, man! That is so confident right there! What you just said is so intelligent. You're very smart young man! Do you think or believe that victims of bullying become violent outcast criminals of society?

Yes, I do. Some people say it doesn't but it's all linked to friendships and relationship and relationships lead to this influence.

Man, that is so true... so true. Please elaborate in your own words, utilizing your own experiences of your life, explaining the connection between bullying and a criminal lifestyle?

Yes, due to the fact that I began fighting and lashing out in the same manner of abuse that was inflicted upon me. You know, so many young people are going through what we have. Right now, as we speak there is a child, teen, young adult being bullied, being abused, and because of this fact, here's the reason for this book. We had to tell our stories. So, the world can see how bullying and abuse really affect people. Bullying and a criminal lifestyle are the same things. The roots come from the beginning of the same thinking... Does someone care? So, we begin lashing out for attention, then find ourselves alone in a lifestyle of criminality.

Okay, that was good. That was really good. That was a great answer. Can you please explain the effects and problems that you experienced as a child or young teen such as a frustration and not being able at communicating with your peers, adults, or your parents?

Of course, I would tell my parents how I'd feel and my stepfather would laugh and ridicule me as being soft and tell me to man up! My parents never supported my healthy lifestyle, so I would lash out saying things to stop my mother and my stepfather that I didn't mean! I started taking things into my own hands and out of control.

Sadly, this is a truth that a lot of our young people are experiencing in their own homes - where they're supposed to be safe and comforted. Instead, they're being pushed down even more. And this hurts me to my soul. This is so sad when a child doesn't feel safe or loved in their own home. There is nowhere else for that child to turn, and it's just an empty, bad feeling of hopelessness – is what leads most children to the streets, gangs, drugs, and ultimately prison! Let's get back to our interview.

Can you explain the behaviors or attitude that you developed as a direct cause of the bullying experiences in your life as a young youth?

I had an "I don't care" attitude. I'm going to do what I want to do. I don't care if I die. I'll live the way that I want to live. My family doesn't love me the way my friends do. I developed the will I live to see the next day type of attitude, which basically summed up to not caring about nothing.

This type of attitude, this type of thinking is exactly why a young teen or young adult starts running with gangs. They feel loved by their friends and not by their families. You have been giving me some really great answers, Mr. Vladimir. Your story is exactly what this book needs. Man, I really appreciate you being s front and straight forward. This is exactly what America needs to hear. Let's finish up with our last question. After answering questions 1 through 8, is there anything else you would like to share with the readers and myself regarding bullying or maybe something you would want them to know concerning your views about bullying on our young youth of today?

I think it's worse today than in my time because it's to the point where if someone tells you to jump off a bridge, a person will. Cyber bullying allows a person who is weak, to be strong with reckless behaviors causing negative influences to kill hopes and dreams. Find someone who loves you and cares for you.

This ladies and gentlemen was our last interview. Hopefully you were just as touched as I was. Not just by one, but by all of these individual stories. Before we go to our next chapter, I want to talk about the thinking patterns of each individual. After reading each interview, you can identify how in each one of these stories, violence, frustration and feelings of loneliness turn an innocent little child into an outcast, a monster and ultimately, a menace to society. Before you make your own decision, identify the domino effect.

1. Bullying
2. Fear
3. Frustration
4. Loneliness
5. Anger
6. Guilt

These all led to a child making poor decisions. Now, these are just the feelings on the surface. The deeper feelings and emotions that are at the core of a child are something that you will have to experience on your own.

CHAPTER 7

I WANT TO TALK A LITTLE BIT more about my story. There are certain pieces that I left out from my younger years of being a victim. There is one part in particular that is urging me to share it.

The year was 1990, we had moved to the projects. I'm not sure if this is where my life changed, but this is where the violence started. This is where I had my first fight and several after. I left this and other parts of my story out because some things I am just too ashamed to tell, but it is in my heart to tell this part of my story.

My first year of living in the projects was hell. I was always a target. I do have two older brothers, but they were never around. You already know I have four siblings under me - with two boys over me and two guys under me. I was the middle son and for some reason, the weight of my younger siblings fell on me... watching them, feeding them, and taking them outside to play. We pretty much did everything together, from the park, to walks, riding bikes, playing basketball, going to the store, even chores around the house. We were always together as a family. Me and my brother, Junior, who is five years younger than me, were inseparable.

Pretty much growing up throughout our lives, we were always together more so than anyone else in my family. It was always him and I. This is due to the fact that the other three were younger than me. But I never left them alone; I did everything with my little brothers and sisters. I remember when Junior and I were much younger; my mother called us Double Trouble. As we got older, it was there is Tito, Junior. Junior was the type of little brother that was always right there. What I did, he did.

Sometimes he was a pain in the butt, but I would never leave him alone. I remember one time we were playing in a river, about 20-30 feet wide. I wanted to cross to the other side but Junior was afraid. He was afraid to get into the water. Me, I've always been fascinated with nature. I've always felt this feeling of being one with the outdoors.

So, I convinced my brother into getting into the water with me. Telling him that there is nothing to be afraid of. Seeing that I was having fun, he made his way in, but I could tell he was still scared. I stayed close to him letting him know that it is okay. As he started to loosen up, he forgot about all of his fears and we started playing, jumping up and down, throwing water at each other. We had a ball. When I told him, I wanted to go to the other side, he immediately backed out getting completely out of the water. I remember his exact words.

Tito, I can't swim," so I told him to stay right there while I go across one time. I did remember I did this for two reason; to show my brother that there is nothing to be afraid of and to see how deep it was going across. It was fairly deep in the middle maybe four or five feet, so we were just little boys. I swam back, only having to really swim when I get toward the middle. A few minutes' worth of swimming, it was nothing.

But when I got back, my brother didn't want to go. I wanted to go across for one reason, I wanted to explore this side like literally and he won't leave my side for anything. I grabbed him by his shoulders and told him, "Junior, there are no sharks in rivers. I was just playing with you." Instantly, he got mad and started crying all over again. This is one of the better memories of my life before the streets, drugs, alcohol and violence consumed me. Here comes the part I am ashamed of. I remember for a year straight I got picked on, beat up, bullied and harassed on a daily basis and I wouldn't do anything. I would just walk away with my head down. I didn't want to fight. I just didn't want any problems.

Truth be told, I was scared, I was afraid... but being the adventurous type of kid that I was, that didn't stop me from going outside. I would just do my best to avoid them. Always having my little brother in tow; we would play where they weren't or we would just go outside of the projects. I remember all that changed when they started picking on my little brother.

Whenever we would see them, I would tell Junior to run and we would always run straight home. But Junior couldn't run as fast as I could, so sometimes we would get caught by the bullies and I would have to cradle my brother in my arms, doing my best to protect him so I would receive most, if not all, of the punishment. There were other times when we would start running and I would let him take the lead telling him to run straight home. Don't look back.

Just keep on running and I would stop to face the bullies alone. I knew running at Junior's speed, we wouldn't make it and I didn't like seeing my brother get beat up. I, eventually, worked up the nerve to fight these entire boys, one on one, before I ended up getting jumped a few more times. One time in particular, there was this beautiful Puerto

Rican girl that lived on the other side of the projects. She would always say 'hi' to me whenever she saw me, so one day, I took a deep breath, grabbed a handful of courage and went and knocked on her door and asked if she could come outside. She was only allowed to come out right there in front of her door. She even had a little sister for Junior to play with. We talked for what seemed like hours.

Before leaving, I remember asking her if she wanted to be my girlfriend, she said "YES!" I was so happy walking back home. Me and Junior were talking about everything our little minds could think of, then out of nowhere, we bumped straight into the bullies. I told Junior to run! Run! As fast as you can and right when we got to the fence leading to our apartment, I literally picked

Junior up and threw him over the fence and told him to run straight inside.

Man, the punk ass kids had whiffled bats that day. You ever get beat up by whiffle bat? Those things hurt.

I remember one time Junior and I were walking from the store, we had bread, eggs, some candy and right as we stepped foot into the projects the bullies popped up. It was always the same three punk ass kids. We couldn't run. They caught us off guard. Besides, they were blocking the direction for our apartment, so we had no choice but to walk by. As I walked by, I got a punch in the back of my head. This time, I got mad as hell. I don't know, if it was because I was tired of getting bullied or because I had my little brother with me. I felt like I had to protect him. I wanted to fight.

Needless to say, I got beat up again. The bread and the eggs were ruined. When I made it home, I lied to my mother telling her that I and Junior were playing around and the bread and eggs got ruined. Little did I know, Junior had already told our Mother what happened.

My mother tells me, "It's okay, just go wash up and get ready for dinner." Little did I know, my mother had a trick up her sleeve? Every day after that, my mother started standing around outside, talking with all of the neighbors, being really friendly with everyone. One day, my mother caught me running from the bullies.

My mother, being the strong woman that she was, was telling the kids, "You want to fight my son, okay, my son is going to fight one of you right now." It just so happened, the boy I was afraid of the most stepped forward saying to her, "Your son is nothing but a punk. I will fight him." My mother looked at me and said, "No son of mine is going to be a punk!"

I was afraid, but my mother standing there gave me strength. We start fighting. I remember the boy had me in a headlock and was choking me bad. I remember I started slipping out of consciousness, then out of nowhere, I got a burst of energy and I got lost in the fight. I remember, I hit that kid so hard in the face, he let me go.

Now, I know what you're thinking, what kind of mother would make her 10-year-old son fight? Well, let me tell you something about my mother, first of all, I love my mother more for this experience. My mother is the one person in this world who taught me how to be independent. My mother taught me how to be a man as well as stand on my own two feet.

Secondly, my mother's a French woman and anyone who knows, French women are not the ones to play with. They will beat a man down with a roller, believe me, I've seen it. My mother would grab and whoop one of those little boys just as soon as she would whoop me. She just wanted me to fight first, to stand up for myself and that is the point of me telling you this part of my story. The time for adults correcting each other's children is over.

Adults don't stick together anymore. After I fought, my mother goes to each of the parents of all those little boys and she explains to their parents what their sons were doing to me and my little brother. She also said if it didn't stop, she would whip them little boys the same way she whoops her own children! You know what those parents said? "After you whoop them, I'm going to whoop them again." My mother became good friends with some of the parents in the projects.

Back at home, my mother made me stand straight up, look her in the eyes and told me, you don't run from anybody. You stand and you fight them boys and they will leave you alone. Looking me straight in my eyes she said, "I better not ever catch you running from anyone ever again, you understand me?" My reply was, "Yes, ma'am."

After this, I fought again with the one boy that I was afraid of the most. The same boy I fought the first time. One of my older brothers was there this time and I fought hard. I must have been a natural at fighting, because this time I had that boy on the ground wheeling on him, but I was still afraid. I didn't want to fight, but I remember what my mother told me. So I fought and I fought hard. A few days later I caught one of the boys picking on Junior and I chased him down to the basketball court and I whipped him. I was never fighting for myself. I was only fighting for my mother or my little brother. When it came down to me being alone, I didn't want to fight.

Although the fighting still happened many times, there were still times where kids would pick on me and I wouldn't do anything. I would just walk away until that day when I was just 14. You read that part of my story earlier, but there is one more time that I ran from someone or should I say a group of dudes and this is the last time I ran from someone. Let me tell you the story. I was 16, my cousin and I came across these dudes that, apparently, my cousin had a problem with. But my cousin hauled ass, so I do the same. When I get back home, my uncle is there and he is mad as hell that my cousin ran on me to cover his own ass. But then he tells my uncle that I ran on him, so I stepped outside. I started speaking my mind like a man because this is what I am and I know that and I know that I am. I tell my cousin after me and your father are done; I'm going to put your fuckin' face in the ground for lying on me.

After this experience, I vowed to myself to never run from anyone ever again. Regardless of how many people, guns, or weapons are involved and because of this promise I've been jumped, injured, and bruised many times. I was never going to run from anyone for two reasons. The first was no one was never ever going to challenge my manhood, ever again. The second was no one was never ever going to call me, Vincent A. Savageau, a punk or anything less than a man, ever again! Wow, with that being said I think about another point I want to bring up. Actually, truthfully, I don't know want to say anything about this, but for some reason, it just feels so wrong not to.

What I will elaborate on, is a point I made earlier about the days for adults, especially parents correcting each other's children, being gone. Those days are over with. Parents don't communicate with each other anymore. There is no understanding between adults anymore. At least, not like when I was growing up. All of the parents in the projects knew each other, even when we moved into the inner city. My mother knew the neighbors. It was like everyone knew everyone. I don't know what the outside world is like today. But it seems like parents do not stick together anymore or they just don't care too. I don't know what the reason is for why parents don't stick together anymore, at least this is my opinion. I could be wrong, but either way, it hurts my heart whenever I sit down or watch the news and the head story is a little girl or boy just committed suicide because of bullies or even a child coming to school with weapons, committing vicious acts of violent crime that leave many injured as well as murdered victims.

But in my mind, I knew who the real victim was. My compassion goes out for the loss of all those families that have lost a child due to bullying. My heart also goes out to those families that have lost their child to prison because of bullies, because that child felt like the only way to make the bullying stop, was to force it to stop. My heart goes out to that child. They're not alone. Although they're not right, but neither was I. And that is the reason for this book; nobody wins... all the way around the board.

Thinking about these children makes me think about my life. Why I became violent and the reason for why I did some of the things I've done just to protect myself or to ensure that I was never going to be the victim ever again. What are you going to do about this epidemic, this pestilence, this disease people? It is clear by now that bullying is a real serious problem that is not just going to go away. We need to come up with some type of system, some type of method to be enforced, not just talked about or not just charges being pressed.

We need to prevent bullying from continuing to ruin the lives of others. A lot of people out there really don't care about bullying and it is passed off as just another part of everyday life. Well, when a beautiful little girl or little boy takes their own life, it should never be passed off as a part of everyday life.

I was still struggling with trying to be a good person at the age of 21. But somewhere along the way, I gave up caring about life, people, the world, society, everything. I just stopped caring.

For so many years, I felt like I was lost. Like I didn't exist. I felt inferior. It was like the world was oblivious of me, so in return, I was totally oblivious to the world. People didn't exist to me. I felt more of a connection with the sky than I did to human beings. I would go out of my way to help stray animals, while at the same time, I would walk right by a human being and when it did come to human beings, my only friends were homeless people or drug addicts. I would socialize with these people because I understand the pain. I wanted to help these people more than any people in the world, but I was so traumatized by all of the bullying and violence in my life that I stopped caring about the life itself.

I stopped caring about people, but for some reason, I didn't forget about God. It was as if someone was always speaking to my heart, whispering in my ear, telling me to never give up. I would cry a lot, not knowing who I was crying to or what I was crying for. The tears would just slowly roll down my face. Whenever I thought about the world, people and how everything, everyone is just so mean. Thinking to myself, why we are built this way, and afraid to hold on to what we love and even more afraid of change.

In my heart, I wanted it so bad-this change. I wanted a new life surrounded by new people. But my mind, my mind wouldn't let me. I just couldn't see outside of the box! I only saw what was before my eyes constantly, consistently on a daily basis - looking through the eyes of a lost soul, looking through the eyes of heartache and pain, wishing and hoping for joy in my life. I was turned away by that same pain and I gave up hope for a new life. I stopped wishing upon a star. I accepted my life for what it was and I engaged it with so much hate, because what I wanted, I couldn't have.

I was mad at the world and all of the people in it. Today, I believe I caused myself more pain. I am the only one still suffering. The guilt and the shame of my actions are on my hands. The sins of my life are on me to blame and that is a burden that I don't want the next little girl or boy to bare.

Now, I am going to tell you why I started using alcohol and other drugs. Going through the abuse I suffered from bullying at a very tender, young age, I, eventually, turned toward violence to protect myself. Like I said, something happened to me when I stabbed that little boy.

Something happened to my heart, hearing the cries and screams of my 9-year-old little brother. Being just a little boy myself, the effects were life-changing, and the very next day, I walked outside with a knife in my pocket… going to the laundromat with my four little brothers and sisters to wash clothes. This was a weekly routine, so the bullies knew exactly where I was going to be and how to catch me. I remembered when I get to the laundromat, I had forgotten my sweater, so I ran back to the house. While walking back to the laundromat, the bullies jumped out from behind a bush.

They were the same boys that were beating on my brother. When they jumped out from behind the bush, I immediately pulled out my knife; they turned and started running, so I did the same.

But then I stopped and thought to myself, why am I running, I got the knife so I turned around and started making my way back to the laundromat, walking with the knife still in my hand. When I reach the laundromat, for some reason I stopped and stood in front of the entrance holding my knife in my hand;

just standing there. And I started thinking, those boys ran from me.

They were afraid of me. I immediately felt this sense of power, this feeling made me strong. I felt strength. I felt brave. I remembered there was this old man always sitting outside of the laundromat. I would see this old man all the time, but he never spoke to me before, until this day. Looking at me he asked, "Young man, you okay?" I just looked at him. I wasn't the type to talk to strangers.

Then he says, you might want to put that knife away before the cops come rolling around. Still staring at him, I just put the knife into my pocket and walked inside of the laundromat. I remember the oriental man behind the counter asked me if I was alright.

Being that I was a regular at this laundromat, the oriental knew my face so he was concerned with my safety rather than kicking me out for having a weapon. At least, this is what I believed and still do believe.

I remember, I walked up to my little brother and told him, "Nobody is going to mess with us anymore," and Junior gave me this look as if he knew and understood exactly what I was talking about. I don't know, if it was because of the knife I had in my pocket, but as I was standing there with all four of my little brothers and sisters, I felt like we were safe. I also vowed to protect them from anyone or anything. Watching them play with each other, I felt comforted. I remember, the next day, I went back to the laundromat to see if that old man was sitting outside and he was, he always was. At the time, I really didn't know why or what I was going for. I just wanted to see if he was there. So, as I passed by and he calls out to me.

So, I stopped, turned around and looked at him and he says if you stand up to them boys and fight those boys, they won't bother you anymore. They will leave you alone; all you have to do is stand up to them. They're all just a bunch of punks anyway. I remember what I asked him. I said, "Why do you care?" And it's the funniest thing he said, "Believe it or not, but I once was a young man myself." For some reason, I thought this to be amusing.

Looking at this old grey haired, bearded man, I couldn't imagine him being any other age, nevertheless going through what I was going through at the time. I thought I was the only one in the world who was going through what I was going through. When I started laughing, he asked me, "What is so funny?" Anyway, I started talking to this old man a lot. I would go down to the corner every day or at least whenever I could. I never really talked to this old man about how I felt or the things I went through or any of my problems for that matter.

I, more so, would just listen to the things he had to say about people, life and the streets and this was the problem for me. Never talking to anyone about how I felt or wanted or what I went through or was going through. I was always depressed. I remember, the old man was always drinking and was always talking about everything. I remember I wanted to feel the same way. One day by myself, I gave some random homeless person 5 dollars to go inside of the liquor store and buy me a 22-oz. bottle of beer. After I drank that bottle of beer, I felt so happy. I felt so good; it was like all of stress went away. I wanted to feel like this every day. So, I started selling weed just so I can buy liquor.

Naturally, I stopped coming home. Being afraid of my mother, I didn't want to get caught drinking or selling weed. I would spend the day with my little brothers and sisters posing as just an innocent little kid with them. At night, I would hit the streets, but this only lasted for a year or may a little more. Like I said by the time, I was 15. My mother knew there wasn't nothing she could do with me.

Don't get me wrong, I've always respected my mother, but she could tell by my demeanor, that I wasn't that sweet innocent little boy anymore. Like I said, my older brothers were never there. The first one was locked up for all of my teens and the second one was always in and out of my life, all of my life. I did what I wanted to do. I made my own path; I followed my own direction.

I started hanging with guys twice my age. Eventually, I started smoking weed. Smoking weed was a different type of high from the way alcohol made me feel. Smoking weed made me feel goofy, funny, and relaxed. Everything just seemed so easy after that first high. As I got older, I started experimenting with other drugs like cocaine and ecstasy. These two drugs quickly became my drugs of choice. The type of effect that these two types of drugs had on me was unlike anything I had ever experienced before. Making my senses five or ten times stronger, I felt like I was unstoppable, unbeatable which didn't go good with the chip I already had on my shoulder from all of the bullying and violence.

My temper would go from zero to sixty in less than a second, but I wasn't just some type of out of control type of dude. It was always the right circumstance, the right situation to throttle my temper. I was always on edge and with this type of attitude I became part of, I just didn't realize until I engaged it. So, always wanting to be in control of everything, I developed a lion's mentality. I hope from reading this you can see why I started using alcohol and other drugs. I never spoke to anyone about my feelings or emotions.

I never spoke to anyone about all of the bullying abuse and the depression that I suffered from and the things that I went through and the things I am talking about in this book. This is us just touching the surface of my life, because all of the shame and embarrassment that I lived with. I was just so afraid to talk about it all for fear of being judged or put down even more - Especially by those that I love.

Never having anyone to talk to, to really be myself, I've always felt alone - even when I had best friends. It was just so hard for me to open up to them. I mean how do you talk to someone about your disabilities, especially when all you want to do is fit in, you want to feel accepted? You want to feel like you belong. How do you sit down and tell someone, "Yeah, I was a punk in school?" I used to get spit on, beat up, pushed to the ground, and choked unconscious, milk poured over my face, made a fool in front of the entire school. Yeah, I suffered from speech and language problems, was always called retarded and dumb and was told I would never amount to anything.

How do you sit there as a young teen or an adult and even talk about that? That's not something you have a conversation about. That's something you want to hide away for the rest of your life. Even now, I am only sharing my story with you because I wish to be brave for all those families and people out there who went through what I went through. On top of being inspired and painfully hurt by stories of those sweet innocent little girls and boys who were no longer here with us, all because of bullies.

I tell my story for them, because they inspire me, they encourage me to speak up and speak out and most importantly, to let it all go. Even from beyond the grave, their stories speak to me. Through my story, I am telling so many stories that normally go untold. This is not just my story. "This is our story." If you understand us, then tell your story too and we will all connect together as one.

Victims of bullying, together we will make a change. I remember the point I wanted to make earlier. The point I wanted to bring up, and this is for the men reading this book. Are we to think that being a man is only about being tough, never running from anything?

As I do believe it is that a man should be brave and stand up for themselves. Believing that we are supposed to be these tough, insensitive human beings is a crippling reflection of our thought process as men and what it really means to be a man.

For me, I believed being a man was just about busting someone's face wide open and having girls around me to please me, whenever I wanted or needed it. I got older, and I realized there is so much more to being a man than just money, cars and girls although I never really had money. Yeah, I sold drugs, only just to get by. For me, it wasn't about buying jewelry, cars, and clothes. I was trying to be some Kingpin. I was only famous in my neighborhood for being the one that never backed down. My enemies feared me for what I would do to them.

People loved me for the way I treated them. For me, that's what it was all about, 'respect'. Money was no object to me. I didn't chase money. I really didn't chase anything. What I wanted in my life, I couldn't have, or at least I thought I couldn't have and what I wanted was love, life, and unity. What I wanted was to feel and be treated like a human being, I wanted to be accepted. I didn't feel like a human being from the time I was just a simple little boy, who picked up a knife to defend himself. It wasn't out of bitterness or anger. I just didn't feel like I belonged. I never felt accepted. Before I started standing up for myself, I've been spit on, beaten down to the ground numerous times and harassed on a daily basis. It didn't matter what school

I went to or the neighborhood I lived in. The outcome was always the same.

My mother always thought I was depressed or stressed because of my so-called disabilities. I was depressed, because no matter where I went or what I did I always got picked on and bullied and the teachers at every school didn't have any clue. Some of my teachers, well really, two of my teachers were worse than the students. I was a soft little boy, all I ever wanted was to go to school. I dropped out of school because of bullying, not because I couldn't learn or because I didn't want to learn. From the time I was 10 to the time I was 14 years old, I suffered a lot of abuse from bullying. Then I suffered more from the violence becoming a violent individual myself. I never thought it was cool to be violent or to be mean. I did the things I did out of self-defense, period.

But by the time I hit my early twenties, I was more than just a bully. I was more than just a mean violent person. I was mad at the world. I was challenging anyone inside or outside of my circle, male or female and if you couldn't live up to my expectations then you couldn't hang with me. I became a lion, the lion being my favorite feline. With that being said, I became a mean vicious bully without even realizing it, without even knowing it. I became what I hate most in life—a bully. Pressure pops up. When it's time, you will either go one way or the other. You are going to make a choice and the decision that you make is going to be based on what you know, based on what you see with your feelings and emotions combined there is nothing in between; you will choose. This is the life that I chose. Now, I have to follow this road.

There are so many little boys and girls out there who will choose like me. There are so many little boys and girls that have already chosen this life that I have chosen and there are so many little girls and boys out there that have killed themselves, "ALL BECAUSE OF BULLYING."

Ultimately, everyone becomes violent. Whether toward themselves or others there is no escaping the bully-everyone conforms, transforms, or just ends it all. The bullies' price will be paid, "either way". It's time now for us to put the bully in its grave!

CHAPTER 8

THERE'S NO OTHER WAY to put it. Bullying is a disease. Full blown. It is a highly infectious disease, one capable of spreading with uncomfortable and harmful intent. I know this to be factual and true because when I was a young boy in school, there was a boy just a bit bigger than myself. Let's say his name is Joe. Let us again say he was an only child. Maybe he was, maybe he was not. But each day he thought it is a good idea to put me in the headlock, push on me or whatever. Now, my caregiver taught me that school is for learning, not horse playing, acting out or anything of that nature. I tried with each to follow suit with this. When is enough, enough?

When I decide to shut down and battle all of the anger up inside until I burst and react in a manner that is unhealthy. I couldn't go to the teacher; I thought that would make me a snitch, a tattletale. Maybe, just maybe if I ignored him, he would disappear. But, no, he didn't disappear, instead, things got worse. With each day, this kid grew more comfortable with his bullying tactics - So comfortable that his own school work was no longer of importance. I was his priority. See, it wasn't that our teacher turned a blind-eye, Joe was just a slickster.

A couple of times I can recall her telling him to keep his hands to himself. Not once realizing that she had never been seeing any of what I'd been going through. This form of behavior in bullying begins to take a toll on you. Also, it affects each individual in different ways. Some become shallow and withdrawn or some even go as far as the thought of or even committing suicide. That's why it is very important to know and pay attention to your child. One never knows what their child is or could be going through on a daily basis.

We must develop a relationship with our children, that way when this type of activity occurs, they're not afraid to bring it home. Communication is definitely the factor here. Us as parents have to first take the initiative at building a healthy form of communication with our children at an early age. We have to step up and initiate conversation in repetition early on. Asking them how was school? Did they learn anything? What they liked or disliked about a certain subject? And this should be done daily so that the lines of communication are open. It's also common for children to shy away from this when they feel uncomfortable about a situation.

One day, Joe caught me down bad with his aunties. He had been drilling me for weeks, maybe months. I actually used to dread going to school. I used to see this boy in my dreams. Then one day, all of the name calling, the pushing, the punches, it all came to a head. I can remember him putting gum in my hair. Again, this was the second time and I had a curl. My mother nearly killed me the first time it happened. When I put my hand in the back of my head and felt that gum, it ignited something in me. I could no longer take the abuse. I stood up.

When I faced Joe, he had this grin on his face that irked me before I knew what I was doing. I had closed my eyes and charged him like I was a bull and he a matador. The impact caused his desk to flip over and we nearly flew five to ten feet across the floor. I had no time to think about what I was doing. Before I knew it, I was on top of Joe wailing on him. The teacher was so shocked at the unexpected behavior she stood frozen for a second.

The reason for me sharing such information was not to promote fighting or glorify violence at all. But to teach our youth that they can't wait until it's too late. You have to express these emotions. Expose these bullies. There's nothing wrong with approaching an adult. That may be the very thing that could save your life. This is something very serious and should be dealt with in the beginning.

It's not the subject that is delicate or fragile. It is your life. And that alone should be taken seriously at all cost.

As I sit here and reminisce back to the very day that I pushed Joe and started hitting him, I can't help but feel a certain type of way. I remember the look on Joe's face, the look on those around me. I felt a sense of courage or relief. I went from being afraid to standing up for myself. I was afraid to tell anyone. I didn't know how to express that someone was picking on me. I didn't have anyone in the home that I could talk to. Communication wasn't a happening thing in my home. I was scared of my own mother. But today, I talk to her about any and everything that I can. The relationship that I so desired, from her, I went after it as I got older and matured.

I address the readers head on about bullying because I never imagined myself going from victim to being the victimizer. I even lost relationships due to my overbearing aggression and bullying ways. I went wrong and I was on a fast track to self-destruction. I would try to control every action, every decision. When things didn't go my way, I even began to use manipulation to bully whoever was on the other end of the incident.

People can look at bullying as only a physical thing, but when you pick at someone who may be more relaxed or not as active and aggressive as yourself, it is a means of mental or emotional bullying.

This too is hurtful and wrong. I failed miserably in doing this because the bullying led me to be physical and aggressive at times. In many situations, now, today, I have reached the decision that emotionally, mentally, and physically bullying someone is cowardice and a scared act and it's time for us to man up and deal with the real issue at hand. Anyone who finds it fun, appealing or gets a laugh out of such malicious and harmful acts are eluding the real issue in their life and are only making room for their downfall.

There are not any help groups that are set up to deal with this type of problem. And I stress the word problem due to the types of actions revolving around bullying today. If you are bullying or even know someone that is being bullied, please address the issue with sincerity. Save a life, express a thought and or even gain a friend.

Life is full of purpose. Learn what yours may be. Too many years go by and time is lost and sense of direction becomes hindered due to us giving unnecessary energy into making someone else feel lost, abused, or even unwanted.

A friend of mine, let's say his name is Jeff. He approached me one day while at work on our lunch break. He addressed me in a cordial manner and gave me criticism that was constructive. He also informed me that what I thought was a game of cracking jokes and fun was much more than that. Me doing this on a daily basis was causing some major issues with this certain individual. Jeff explained to me that the person-in-question had missed 2 days of work and that occurred due to my constant badgering.

With careful intent, I listened and he was done, I felt the lowest of anything low on earth and maybe even lower than that.
To learn that this man nearly overdosed stunned me and had me speechless. My using him as a pass-time or whatever was actually humiliating and hurtful. His already low self-esteem had plummeted to the lowest grade of all self-worth.

At hearing this, I began to feel nearly the same. To know my antics were the cause of his accident did something to me. Most of all, it made me realize that I was far from joking. I was picking on this man even during some of my so-called sessions when I did recognize that he was hurt beyond what I was doing. I still continued. I took that he wasn't like me or even as strong as myself for granted. Now, today I am more aware of the next person's feelings.

My situation taught me a valuable lesson. It isn't right, nor is it fair to make someone or anyone (for that matter) feel any type of discomfort.

They deserve more than that. In 2014, I am more aware. I know the difference between joking and bullying. And I don't go overboard with the joke time.

During all of this, I was able to go back in my life and remember when I myself had not always been among the most popular. I wasn't "The Most Popular", but I was average. I was in the Top 3 of the fastest sprinters on our class's field day. I was athletic - A class act. I made the girls laugh, but I had a few guys that taunted me. Even though, I didn't run off and close the closet door or hide out, I did feel a certain type of way. The same way, I made the dude feel.

There's so much that I can say to show and prove my case, so many incidents and I don't dare want to make the mistake of painting a picture as if only children can or are being bullied. Yes, as I have mentioned before, bullying has not only one face, this masked manipulator has many faces not only that, but it has many tactics for which it attacks in many different angles—emotional, physical, mental.

Adults all over the world are affected by this. Some innocent man or female have become victims to another bully's antics.

The time is now... time to take a stand... time to overcome that fear of asking for help. It's time to dig deep, deep down in the soul and grab a hold of the courage that lies there. Get a hold of that courage and address the issue at hand. Doing so can help you help others. Doing so can very well make your burden that much lighter. No one deserves to be bullied. Everyone deserves a fair chance.

I can speak from experience alone. I don't ever want to make any human being feel like life isn't worth living. I am ashamed. I am ashamed. I am remorseful for my actions and I want my readers to understand the significance of what I am saying.

There's nothing macho, nothing tough or manly about picking at someone to the point that they feel useless, helpless and most of all worthless.

There's NOT one thing tough about bullying a human being who may be less aggressive, not as strong or not as smart as you are.

I can say this, though. When the wrong you do to someone else, makes you smile, it's only a matter of time before your smile is turned upside down. The very things that you do to another person can be done to you just the same.

This topic is so important and should be dealt with in the just of matters. There have been so many tragedies over the years and as of late, much more. This leads me to believe that SOMETHING must be wrong, something must be done. Still, I ask the question, how do we correct this from happening? How do we prevent bullying? We develop a system. We attack the core. We teach our youth how to handle or deal with situations when met with this type of behavior. We hold classes. We confront our bullies. So yes, I believe that we take this to group sessions. We give it its necessary attention. We deal with it head-on.

Over my little time for which I had the opportunity to study or look into bullying, I had the chance to learn a few major things.
One - A person who has the characteristics or activities of a bully is deficient with the lack of knowledge and understanding, doesn't recognize their dysfunctional ways.
Two - A person doesn't see that hurt or anger is outward spoken when not dealt with within.

I've also had the opportunity to witness bullying at a weak and low state, as well as at full throttle. Both ways, an individual is affected by these actions. I'll tell you this. Both victim and victimizer have the opportunity to seek help, reach out to a bully prevention group in your area.

Talk to the closest person to you. And if you don't have anyone, reach out to your creator. Develop a personal relationship with your Lord.

It's time to address the issue. It's time that we shed light over the dark shadows that haunt our well-being.

Today, I say to you this. Together, we are able to overcome any all obstacles. Don't be afraid any longer. Fear God alone; do not let one thing hinder you from the happiness you deserve. Although, we have touched on a few things revolving around bullying, I'm here to tell you that in doing so, we have barely, barely scratched the surface. There is so much more to be discussed. There is so much more to learn about. One thing is for certain, we have touched on the basics. We are getting it out in the open, confronting it, talking about it.

I express to you in all sincerity. With me talking about bullying, many emotions flock to me, causing me to be overwhelmed with feeling emotions that relate back to the beginning. The times when I was unable to go to someone and tell them I was having an issue at school, the park, or wherever... then the time where I see the power in standing up for myself.

Then too, when the very things that had me shocked, I began to put others through. I'm sure that I have a story much like many. The circumstances may be alike, or even different, but bullying, in any manner is cowardice and the person who thinks it makes them stronger, tougher, or more

dominant, they are the losers. They're the ones scared to face what's really going on.
I'm near forty-years and still maturing. I'm calling all bullies on this. Put yourself in your victim's shoes. Try to walk in them. Visualize yourself being shamed, made to feel like nothing... helpless...afraid. Can you see it? No, for real, really step out on the ledge. What, are you scared? Of course, you are.

You don't want to feel weak. Why are you afraid that someone may start to take advantage of you? Now, you see how others feel.

Remember, I told you this. Where someone is strong, there is always someone stronger. When you commit wrong, it is natural that you're wrong, so there is a debt. And eventually, that debt has to be paid. Have you ever heard of KARMA? She's no relation to superstition. She's related to just due and her payment will be collected in full. It might not be today or tomorrow, but she's going to definitely collect.

Can you picture your child being afraid or scared to come to you for help or advice? Picture your child bully. Can you see yourself vulnerable and unable to protect your child from your duty and title claims? How about your child causing such discomfort to another child? Do you continue to allow this to go on? Or do you step up to the bat and take a swing at an issue that is causing so much heartache in our society? Be the parent that becomes the director of the solution.

CHAPTER 9

BULLYING AND HOW IT AFFECTED ME

BULLYING AFFECTED ME mentally, causing depression, frustration, anxiety, and low self-esteem. Bullying caused me to make poor decisions early in my life - Decisions that would affect me later on in my life. Decisions like dropping out of high school, using alcohol and other drugs at an early age - Using violence to express myself instead of communicating my feelings or frustrations... decisions that lead me to a poor and unhealthy lifestyle - Decisions that lead me to develop poor character and unethical social skills. The side effects of bullying left me feeling sad and alone most of the time. Never learning how to properly express myself made me not care or even want to. I would just keep all of my embarrassment, shame, guilt, and secrets locked up inside of me. The side effects of which left me feeling anti-social, never really wanting to talk to people. Not out of hate, but because I developed low self-esteem. I was afraid people would judge me and look at me like I was weak.

The mental and physical traumas of bullying: First, let me say the bullying experiences in my life were devastating. I received drastic bullying for four years of my life. From 10 years old up until 14 years old. I remember for a year straight, I got bullied on a daily basis... from school to the bus ride home or in my own neighborhood. A day did not go by where I didn't receive some type of bullying. Sometimes, it would come in the form of words where other times, it would get physical. But let's talk about the physical traumas first. Like black eyes, bruised ribs and busted lips, all from bullies, starting at the age of 10 years old.

The abuse I suffered from bullying had a dramatic effect on me mentally, especially being so young; it was overwhelming, playing itself hard on me. Mentally, I became paranoid, full of fear and depression, struggling with low self-esteem, battling with the negative thoughts that I believed of myself. Thoughts like I will never be good enough, smart enough, always telling myself I would never amount to anything. When all I ever wanted was to be something or someone great! I would always wish upon a star. But I was defeating myself because I believed the entire put downs that those negative people in my life were saying. The mental effects caused me to live in a shell, living in a little box of a life while other teens were happy going to school with all of their friends. I was in the streets, learning and developing that type of lifestyle that turns a young girl or boy into nothing that is sweet or innocent. Today, I have a profound understanding of myself versus when I was just a little boy, but that doesn't mean I don't deal with bullying anymore. I am in prison, which is a school yard for bullies. I am an expert now when dealing with these types of mentality or behavior, but the mental effects are still there. They are still the same - People trying to fill you with fear. The difference is, I am an adult now and I take the necessary time to educate myself and learn about myself.

So, today I can be extremely confident and I learned how to control my feelings/emotions a long time ago. I stopped letting people get me outside of my character or my body a long time ago. I am the ruler of me. Bullying will never go away. Like one of my interviewees said, bullying is something you deal with at all ages. We deal with bullies all of our lives. They come in any shape, form, or fashion. My lion's mentality is something I will live with for the rest of my days. This mentality is deeply inputted into my brain. How serious is bullying? Bullying is more than what people think or know, even for that average kid who got picked on in Junior or High School and is now an attorney or business owner.

The bullying is rooted deep within the mind, somewhere hidden in the subconscious and this type of behavior whether fear or aggression is unconsciously passed down to the children. Without even knowing it or realizing it, you can tell your child, through your conduct, to be either afraid or aggressive.

Sometimes you can look at someone and determine from their persona what type of person they are and/or if they were the class clown, bully, nerd or victim. Nerd and victim go hand in hand. With that being said, I can almost nine times out of ten tell if someone was a victim of bullying at some point in time in their life. Why? Because the effects of bullying never leave you, and unconsciously, this disease can and will spread to your family before your child even starts school. Based on your attitude, your conduct and your actions, your child will be either one or the other. There is no between when it comes to a bully. In conclusion, there are tools that can be applied to help defeat the effects of bullying and those tools can possibly prevent some bullying from damaging our young. So, let's go through the tools again. I call these tools the 4 Power Tools of communicating, knowing, learning, and teaching. Remember what I said in chapter 3 about utilizing these tools. Applying these tools effectively can make all the difference in your family, as well as in your personal life.

But some of the most important things for a child are confidence, self-esteem, a healthy attitude, a healthy mind, self-defense, and boundaries all applied with tender, love and care and you have yourself a healthy child or children. What is the ultimate responsibility? Family!

How do we work through the family? Through awareness, sensitivity, sympathy, empathy, and acceptance. The most important of all these is "empathy." Understanding is the key, so with that, understand yourself, your family and all of those people in your life, in your child's life and everything around you and you will personally succeed better and far greater in your life.

CHAPTER 10

THE DIFFERENT TYPES OF BULLYING PARENTS SHOULD WATCH FOR

1. PHYSICALY BULLYING

This occurs when someone uses physical actions (such as kicking, slapping, shoving, hitting, punching) to gain power and control over their targets. This is the most obvious form of bullying and is the easiest to identify.

People who physically bully tend to be bigger, stronger, and more aggressive.

Because this is the easiest form to identify, historically, it has received more attention from schools than other forms of bullying.

2. VERBAL BULLYING

Verbal bullies usually use insults to belittle, demean, and hurt another person. They use words, statements, and name-calling to gain control and power over a target, which they often base on the way they look, act, or behave. Verbal bullies also commonly target kids with special needs.

Unlike physical bullying, verbal bullying is often difficult to identify because attacks commonly occur when someone in authority isn't around, which leads to having one's word against another's.

3. EMOTIONAL BULLYING

Also referred to as relational aggression, this type of bullying often goes unnoticed by parents and teachers. It is a type of social manipulation wherein a person tries to hurt someone else or to sabotage their social standing, often by ostracizing others from a particular group, spreading rumors, manipulating situations, and breaking their confidence.

The goal of the bully is to increase their own social standing at the expense of bullying another person.

4. CYBERBULLYING

With teens and tweens always being connected in this digital age, cyberbullying is a growing problem among young people. It is also becoming more prevalent because bullies can harass their targets with much less risk of getting caught. Examples of cyberbullying include posting hurtful images, creating online threats, and sending hurtful emails or text messages.

Cyberbullies often say things they don't have the courage to say face to face. Technology makes them feel anonymous, isolated, and oblivious to the situation. For victims of cyberbullying, it feels invasive and endless. Bullies can reach them anytime, anywhere, often in the safety of their own home. Therefore, the consequences of cyberbullying are significant.

5. SEXUAL BULLYING

Sexual bullying consists of repetitive, harmful, and degrading acts directed at a person. Examples include sexual name-c, rude comments, vulgar gestures, sexual name-calling, touching without consent, sexual propositions, and pornographic material. A bully may make a rude comment about a person's appearance, attractiveness, sexual development, or sexual activity.

In extreme cases, this type of bullying opens the door to sexual assault. Girls are often subjected to sexual harassment by both boys and other girls. Sexting can also open doors to sexual harassment (e.g. when girl sends an intimate photo of her to her partner, it can easily be spread widely after a breakup, which may then lead her to become a target of sexual harassment when people make fun of her body and call her names).

6. PREJUDICIAL BULLYING

This type of bullying is based on prejudices people have towards someone of a different race, religion, and sexual orientation, and this type encompasses all other types of bullying. Those who bully prejudicially target others who are different from them and singling them out.

10 WAYS TO PREVENT BULLYING

1. BEGIN AT HOME

As parents, it is important to educate your children on what bullying really is. It is vital for them to understand not just the definition of bullying, but also what it looks and feels like because bullying, as we have tackled previously, comes in many forms. Start by explaining what a healthy friendship is like and what is not.

Research suggests that parents are usually the last to know when their child is being bullied, but you can break that trend by talking to your kids daily about school and what's happening in their social lives. It is important to ask questions that are engaging and open-ended:

- Who did you play with at recess?
- What was the hardest thing you did today?
- When I went to school there were some mean kids that were kind of mean and used to tease other kids, have you noticed anything like that at your school?
- What's something good that happened today?

2. LEARNING WARNING SIGNS

Most children won't tell anyone when they have been bullied or being bullied, so it is vital that you recognize the warning signs that your child is being bullied:

- Avoiding school or activities
- Changes in eating habits
- Changes in hygiene
- Grades are dropping
- Experiencing headaches, stomachaches, and other illnesses.
- Changes in mood and personality

3. INSTILL HEALTHY HABITS

More than just teaching your children on what bullying is like, it is also important to instill an anti-bullying mindset in them. This not only includes teaching your children not to hit, shove, or tease other kids, but also teaching them that being critical, judgmental, making hurtful jokes, and spreading rumors also are unhealthy and constitute bullying.

It is also vital to teach your children about responsible online behavior because cyberbullying, as previously mentioned, is a big issue in the digital age.

4. EMPOWER YOUR CHILDREN

Alongside educating your children, one of the most helpful things you can do as a parent is to provide them with tools for dealing with bullying. Here are some tools that you can share with them:

- Walk away from the bully
- Tell an adult about the incident
- Tell the bully in a firm voice to stop

It is also crucial to teach them when and how to report an incident of bullying when they witness one as it is important for the to understand that they shouldn't be a bystander when bullying takes place.

5. BECOME FAMILIAR WITH YOUR SCHOOL'S POLICIES

Another important thing you can do as a parent is to know how bullying is handled at your child's school, which includes knowing who to call if something happens with your children and knowing what to expect for how the situation will be handled.

6. REPORT BULLYING INCIDENTS

In the case that your child tells you that s/he is being bullied, make sure that you start by contacting school personnel and ask to meet with them in person to demonstrate that you're committed to seeing that the issue is resolved.

Documenting all bullying incidents is also helpful so you can be prepared if the situation escalates and law enforcement or other outside sources need to be involved.

7. BE AN ADVOCATE

While it's vital to become an advocate for bullying prevention, it's also important to offer your time by volunteering to work with teachers and guidance counselors to develop an anti-bullying program to take your advocacy a step further. In case you child's school doesn't have a program yet, initiate events and fundraisers to jumpstart the school's anti-bullying campaign.

8. RECRUIT OTHER PARENTS

Form a group of parents who are willing to commit to the bullying prevention program in order for it to be more successful. Regularly meet with them to brainstorm ideas, plan engaging events, and help in putting new plans/suggestions into action.

9. SPEND MORE TIME AT SCHOOL

If you have the extra time, volunteer at school functions for additional adult supervision because this is, oftentimes, enough to prevent bullying.

10. ASK THE PTA/PTO TO SPONSOR A BULLYING-PREVENTION PROGRAM

In case your child's school has limited funds for bullying programs, you may approach your local PTA/PTO to ask for assistance. This may help you in putting up a fundraiser to raise awareness and money for the program.

THANK YOU FOR READING my story. Thank you for your time and be an advocate for "NO BULLIES ALLOWED!"

Fight the good fight, raise awareness and let's put an end to this disease we call bullying and make our land a better country to live in.

I love you all.

Sincerely,
Vincent A. Savageau

HOTLINES:

- *National Suicide Hotline:* 1-800-SUICIDE (784-2433)
- *National Suicide Prevention Lifeline:* 1-800-273-TALK(8255)

These are both toll-free, 24-hour confidential hotlines which connect you to a trained counselor at the nearest suicide crisis center.

- *Project Safe Place:* 1-888-290-7233

Project Safe Place provides access to immediate help and supportive resources for young people in crisis through a network of qualified agencies, trained volunteers and businesses in 32 states.

Call the hotline to find out if the program operates in your state.

- *National Alliance of the Mentally Ill*: 1-800-950-6264

Toll-free, confidential hotline operating Monday to Friday, 10 am to 6 pm (EST). Trained volunteers provide information, referrals, and support to anyone with questions about mental illness.

- *The Trevor Project:* 866-4-U-TREVOR

The Trevor Project operates the only nationwide, around-the-clock crisis and suicide prevention helpline for lesbian, gay, bisexual, transgender, and questioning (LGBTQ) youth. The Trevor Helpline is available as a resource to parents, family members and friends of young people as well.

Visit www.TheTrevorProject.org for more information and resources for young people, including "Dear Trevor," an online Q&A forum for non-time sensitive questions.

- *Another Chance 4 Youth, Inc.*

A Nationwide Youth nonprofit dedicated to helping tomorrow's youth today! www.ac4y.org

NOTE TO READERS: If you or someone that you know has been bullied, needs help and support, please do not hesitate to follow up with some of the resources above, or contact us at ac4y.org or at 843-879-8361.

YOU ARE NOT ALONE!

I am glad I don't look like what I've been through.

A mind is a terrible thing to waste.

Programming is priceless.

Certificate of Completion

VINCENT SAVAGEAU

HAS SUCCESSFULLY COMPLETED THE FOLLOWING
ACE COURSE

SPANISH

GIVEN AT U.S.P. McCREARY THE 21ST DAY OF
AUGUST IN THE YEAR 2008

_____ _____
M. CASADA   G. BOGGS, SOE

Certificate of Completion

VINCENT SAVAGEAU

HAS SUCCESSFULLY COMPLETED THE FOLLOWING
ACE COURSE

ESSAY WRITING

GIVEN AT USP McCREARY THIS 1ST DAY OF JUNE IN
THE YEAR 2010

_____ _____
G. HOLLIS   G. BOGGS, SOE

Certificate of Completion

Vincent Savageau

HAS SUCCESSFULLY COMPLETED THE FOLLOWING
ACE COURSE

LEADERSHIP

GIVEN AT U.S.P. McCREARY THE 21ST DAY OF
JUNE IN THE YEAR 2012

_____ _____
R. McCAFFREY   G. BOGGS

Certificate of Completion

Vincent Savageau

HAS SUCCESSFULLY COMPLETED THE FOLLOWING
ACE COURSE

Effective Communication

GIVEN AT U.S.P. McCREARY THE 13TH DAY OF
FEBRUARY IN THE YEAR 2013

_____ _____
R. McCAFFREY   G. BOGGS

UNITED STATES PENITENTIARY MCCREARY

Certificate of Achievement

Savageau, Vincent

Completion of
Victim Impact Class

April 2, 2013

M. Lawson, Counselor

Certificate of Completion

Awarded to

Vincent Savageau

for successfully completing the Orientation curriculum of the
Challenge Program at U.S.P. McCreary

Presented on the 21st day of June 2013

K. Smith
K. Smith, Challenge Treatment Specialist

J. Figueroa, Psy. D.
Challenge Coordinator

Certificate of Completion

Vincent Savageau

HAS SUCCESSFULLY COMPLETED THE FOLLOWING ACE COURSE

Effective Communication

GIVEN AT U.S.P. McCREARY THE 11TH DAY OF JULY IN THE YEAR 2013

R. McCAFFREY G. BOGGS

Challenge Program Award

Certificate of Completion

to

Vincent Savageau

for

Rational Thinking Journal in Challenge Program at USP McCreary

Presented on July 26, 2013

J. Booker J. Figueroa PSY. D
Challenge Treatment Specialist Challenge Coordinator

Certificate of Completion

Awarded to

Vincent Savageau

for successfully completing
Reviewing My Drug Use
at
United States Penitentiary McCreary
CHALLENGE Program

Completed on the 30th day of August 2013

_____
M. Anderson
Challenge Treatment Specialist

_____
J. Figueroa Psy.D.
Challenge Coordinator

Certificate of Achievement

Awarded to

Savageau

12746-021

For Runner-Ups In The
1st Annual Kickball Tournament

USP McCreary, Pine Knot, KY
September 2013

_____
D. Riney
Recreation Specialist

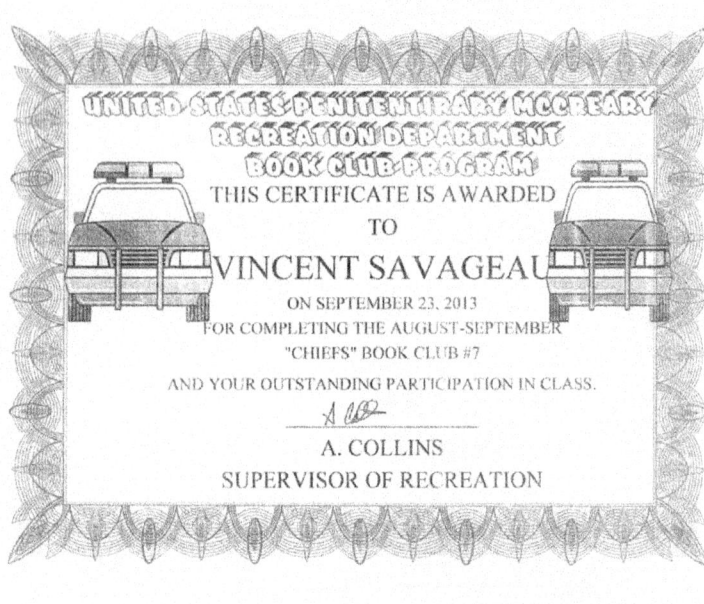

UNITED STATES PENITENTIARY MCCREARY
RECREATION DEPARTMENT
BOOK CLUB PROGRAM

THIS CERTIFICATE IS AWARDED

TO

VINCENT SAVAGEAU

ON SEPTEMBER 23, 2013

FOR COMPLETING THE AUGUST-SEPTEMBER
"CHIEFS" BOOK CLUB #7

AND YOUR OUTSTANDING PARTICIPATION IN CLASS.

A. COLLINS
SUPERVISOR OF RECREATION

Participant of the Month

Awarded to

Vincent Savageau

for consistently displaying the
Eight Positive Attitudes
at

**United States Penitentiary McCreary
CHALLENGE Program**

Presented during the month of

September 2013

M. Anderson
Challenge Treatment Specialist

J. Figueroa Psy.D.
Challenge Coordinator

Certificate of Completion

Awarded to

Vincent Savageau

for successfully completing the Criminal Lifestyles curriculum of the Challenge Program at U.S.P. McCreary

Presented on the 4th day of October 2013

_____
K. Smith, Challenge Treatment Specialist

_____
J. Figueroa, Psy. D.
Challenge Coordinator

UNITED STATES PENITENTIARY MCCREARY
RECREATION DEPARTMENT
BOOK CLUB PROGRAM

THIS CERTIFICATE IS AWARDED

TO

VINCENT SAVAGEAU

ON OCTOBER 30, 2013

FOR COMPLETING THE SEPTEMBER-OCTOBER
"ENDER'S GAME" BOOK CLUB #8

AND YOUR OUTSTANDING PARTICIPATION IN CLASS.

A. COLLINS
SUPERVISOR OF RECREATION

Challenge Program Award

Certificate of Completion

to

Vincent Savageau

for

Violence Prevention Journal in Challenge
Program at USP McCreary

Presented on November 20, 2013

J. Booker
Challenge Treatment Specialist

J. Figueroa PSY.D
Challenge Coordinator

Certificate of Completion

Awarded to

Vincent Savageau

for successfully completing
Communication Skills
at
United States Penitentiary McCreary
CHALLENGE Program

Completed on the 17th day of December 2013

M. Anderson
Challenge Treatment Specialist

J. Figueroa Psy.D.
Challenge Coordinator

Certificate of Completion

Awarded to

Vincent Savageau

for successfully completing
Lifestyle Balance
at
United States Penitentiary McCreary
CHALLENGE Program

Completed on the 24th day of January 2014

L. Howard
Challenge Treatment Specialist

J. Figneton Psy.D.
Challenge Coordinator

BULLYING

ORDER FORM

$12.99
+ $5.50 SHIPPING FEE

CALL LOCAL:
843-879-8361
www.anotherchancemedia.org

Another Chance Media
P.O. Box 78
Mullins, SC 29574

PAYMENT OPTIONS:

Send check or money order to:

ANOTHER CHANCE MEDIA
P.O. BOX 78
MULLINS, SC 29574

Please indicate book name and quantity

Name: _____ Number: _____

Email: _____

Mailing Address: _____

_____

Book Order: _____

_____

TOTAL: _____

www.ingramcontent.com/pod-product-compliance
Lightning Source LLC
Chambersburg PA
CBHW032038090426
42744CB00004B/55